Pastor Daniels Ekarte
and the
African Churches Mission
Liverpool 1931-1964

Marika Sherwood

With a preface by Stephen Small

HANSIB

Published in Great Britain by Hansib Publications in 2023

Hansib Publications Limited
76 High Street, Hertford, SG14 3WY, UK

info@hansibpublications.com
www.hansibpublications.com

First published by The Savannah Press in 1994

Cover: Painting of Pastor Daniels Ekarte, reproduced with the kind permission of the artist, Joseph Ankrah, son of Reginald Ankrah, choirmaster and organist at the Mission

ISBN 978-1-7393211-7-8
ISBN 978-1-7393211-8-5 (Kindle)
ISBN 978-1-7393211-9-2 (ePub)

A CIP catalogue record for this book
is available from the British Library

Design & Production by Hansib Publications Ltd
Printed in Great Britain

This book is dedicated to the women of the South End of Liverpool, whose courage, strength and perseverance I glimpsed in the course of researching a book about a man and his mission.

The opening of the African Churches Mission, 1931
(By courtesy of Reeves/NMGM)

Acknowledgements

WITHOUT THE INFORMATION GIVEN TO ME BY MANY people this small book could not have been written and the memory of Pastor Daniels Ekarte might have died with the last of those who knew him. This has been the fate of many Black women and men (and working-class people) whose work should be known and whose life should be celebrated and enshrined in the pages of history. I wish to acknowledge my debt to:

Addy Ankrah
Mrs V. Charnod
Grace Heard
Marie and Charlie Jenkins
Mr Johnson
Nathaniel Laryea
Mr T. McKavitt
Mrs M. O'Brien
Philip Osisiogu
James Phillips
Rose Phillips
Rita Reeves
Mr & Mrs S. Rogers
Sam Scotland
Dave Young

Thank you. There is more than a debt. The whole Ankrah family has offered me friendship and made me welcome in the family home in Liverpool. Addy Ankrah and Rita Reeves especially gave up much of their time to talk to me and to respond to my many questions. I hope this book will not disappoint them. For everybody's patience with an ignorant London-based Hungarian I shall never find the appropriate words to express my gratitude.

Without the bed offered by Marij van Helmond on my many trips to Liverpool, and also by Addy Ankrah and Lynn and Dave Marks I could not have done the work. I want also to thank Marij for her patience with my frequent Ekarte-obsession while I was her guest, and for her interest and support. Also Teajer Carson at Hector Peterson Court for her help and ready hospitality.

The following people gave their time to read and comment on the manuscript: David Abdullah, Addy and Edmund Ankrah, Mike Boyle, Wally Brown, Ray Costello, Joe Farraq, Adam Hussein, Dorothy Kuya, Rose Phillips, Colin Prescod, Rita Reeves, Steve Small and Marij van Helmond. Though our views have not always coincided, I benefited greatly from your comments. Thank you.

Finally I must thank my son Craig Sherwood for reading and correcting the final version, and my brother Andrew Fenyo for typesetting the book.

Marika Sherwood
London, 1994

ACKNOWLEDGEMENTS TO THE NEW PRINTING

This would not have been possible without substantial support and contributions by several people. I would like to thank Tayo Aluko, who played an important role in helping reprint this book, including proof-reading part of the manuscript and writing the back cover synopsis. I would like to thank Kash Ali and Hansib Publications for agreeing to the reprint and for working so hard to bring it to fruition. And finally, most of all, I would like to thank my dear friend Stephen Small, for kick-starting the process of reprinting the book, for proof-reading part of the manuscript, for writing a preface to the new edition and for the substantial financial contribution he made to paying for the reprint.

Marika Sherwood, 2023

Contents

APPENDICES

Preface

THIS HISTORY OF PASTOR DANIELS EKARTE AND THE
African Churches Mission is a fascinating account of one man's
struggle to improve the life of a community, regardless of colour,
creed, religion, or nationality and origins. Just to help people
overcome poverty. It's the story of an African immigrant to
Liverpool in the early decades of the 20th century who remained
in the city for the rest of his life. It's a story about race, racism
and resistance in the city of Liverpool during this period. And it's
a story that took place on a larger canvas than the city alone,
because Pastor Ekarte's efforts unfolded when the British empire
in Africa was at its dubious pinnacle – controlling vast amounts
of territory and massive numbers of people. This was a period in
which preaching and pontificating about bringing civilization,
Christianity and culture to Africa's savages was pre-eminent,
most of it little more than a masquerade for plunder, profit and
prestige.

This is the first and only book about Pastor Ekarte and the
African Churches Mission (ACM). The book was first published
in 1994 and we are fortunate that Marika Sherwood found out
about him, met and interviewed men and women who had worked
with him, including many who had been children at the ACM.
She also scoured the archives for insights into his life. Pastor's
Ekarte's life is a story of dedication, determination and
commitment. And Marika's life's work – researching, teaching,
transforming organizations – is also a tale of dedication,
determination and commitment. She very much hopes that many
others will follow in her footsteps, as far more research needs to
be done on Africans here since they arrived with the Roman

conquerors. This book provides an opportunity to recognize her overall contributions. And that's why I'm proud and honoured that she has agreed to reprint the book and to allow me to write this short preface.

Details of Pastor Ekarte's life are scant and almost everything we know about him comes from this book. Ekarte was born in Calabar, Nigeria, around the start of the twentieth century, became involved in Christianity and arrived in Liverpool around 1915. After a personal struggle with gambling and crime, he straightened himself up and began God's work locally. He was able to secure modest funds from a variety of sources and opened the African Churches Mission in 1931 at 122-124 Hill Street. Over the following decades the ACM provided religious and social services to the poor and needy – along with food, clothes and shelter – for women, children and men. He advised Africans and many others who arrived in the city looking for work or housing. The ACM also held special services and events to celebrate holidays and the arrival of guests; and to bring some joy to a community struggling with poverty or debt. In the 1940s the Mission became a home for a number of children, especially those of mixed Black and white parentage, including the so-called 'Brown Babies' abandoned by Black American fathers who were in military service in Liverpool during World War Two.

During his life Ekarte knew a wide range of people, locally, nationally and internationally, and he corresponded and worked with governments, churches, and local and national politicians. These included men and women nationally and internationally important in anti-racism, Pan-Africanism and African independence campaigns, for example George Padmore. Nnamdi Azikiwe, who became the first president of independent Nigeria, knew Ekarte well and sent several of his fellow countrymen to stay at the ACM – he probably stayed there himself. Ekarte also worked with race equality leader Harold Moody of the League of Coloured People and interacted with the West African Students Union, founded in London in 1925. He had probably met Ras Makonnen, who hosted the Pan-African Congress in Manchester in 1945. Ekarte met Paul Robeson at a meeting to welcome him to the city which took place in St. George's Hall in Liverpool in 1948. And Dorothy Kuya was at that meeting. Dorothy Kuya, a local legend, born and raised in Liverpool 8, was a communist, pan-Africanist and later on, from the early 2000s, played a prominent role in the establishment of the International Slavery Museum in Liverpool. Ludwig Hesse, an active pan-Africanist and Dorothy's mentor, was certainly there too, because Hesse helped organize the visit by Robeson. I'm curious about Ekarte's interactions with Hesse and with Kuya; hopefully current work being carried out on Dorothy Kuya's papers will reveal more information. And I wonder if he met Una Marson or Claudia Jones, Black Caribbean women who played important roles in struggles for racial equality in England and across the Diaspora. Kwame Nkrumah, first prime minster of independent Ghana, spent about three weeks in Liverpool in September-October 1935, while on his way to enrol at Lincoln University (USA). He stayed with the Liverpool agent of Ghanaian timber merchant George Grant. In 1945, having completed his studies he was back in the UK, on his way home. But he became involved in some local organizations: he reports in his *Autobiography* (1957, p.58) that 'the work connected with these coloured workers led me on fairly regular visits to Liverpool, Manchester and Cardiff...' In November 1947 he embarked on a ship in Liverpool to take him home to what was then called the Gold Coast. He stayed at the Mission and certainly met Pastor Daniels during at least one of his visits. The African American sociologist and anthropologist, St. Clair Drake, met Ekarte and worked with him on multiple occasions to help find funds for the ACM, in particular with regard to the so-called 'brown babies' in Ekarte's care.

Ekarte spent tireless hours to improve people's lives, but it was a constant struggle and over time he became tired and demoralized. His efforts were stifled, largely by racist opposition. In the end he was worn down. By the end of the 1950s local and national authorities took over some of the services he had provided and bypassed him. The city's Black population became more diverse, demands for African and West Indian independence were growing, and he no longer seemed relevant to their needs. The

ACM building became more dilapidated and was eventually demolished. Ekarte died just a few weeks after that.

Marika's book provides a detailed history of Pastor Ekarte, his life, his activities and most of all his work in creating and sustaining the African Churches Mission. She details his energy and drive, his determination to help those in need and his Christian beliefs. She also details the profound and enduring racism he faced, from the British government, the Liverpool Council, local welfare associations, and several others. For example, he was the victim of verbal abuse from local and national authorities, and harassment from the police, from the Colonial Office and from prominent religious leaders. This new printing of the book has additional information that was not in the first edition, specifically several written reflections on his experiences as a young boy in the ACM, by Thomas J Jones, and a Remembrance Day Calendar with the photograph of Ekarte.

Marika is not shy to confess that she doesn't have all the answers to Ekarte's life. She points out there is a lot we don't know and that there are many records that the British government and organizations have destroyed or say they don't have. But she makes suggestions about where we can find more information.

There are several reasons why this book is important, especially right now in 2023. It's important because it's a detailed, no-punches-pulled account of the life of a working class African immigrant, who arrived in England early in the 20th century, and dedicated his life to helping others. It's important because the information comes from people in the Liverpool 8 multi-racial community who lived and worked and contributed to his work and who benefited from it. It's important because it provides insights into a community leader who was not internationally famous, who did not write books and treatises that future generations would read, and who did not lead an international organization, or become head of an African state. In this regard it broadens and expands our knowledge of the people that did not become famous, but whose work is indispensable in the quest for social justice. And it's important because it brings to light important information about Liverpool and its Black and multi-racial community.

In fact, the reprinting of this book is very timely. Since the murder of George Floyd in 2020, the mobilization of multi-racial groups and individuals across Great Britain to remove or rename statues, to return precious museum artefacts and to decolonize education and knowledge production, has led to institutions beginning to pay attention and even take some action. But before we jump the gun, let's be clear – these are baby steps not giant strides. They've opened up far more than ever before, but still nowhere near as much as we deserve. The streets, the museums and university halls are ringing with calls for social justice and for a more accurate, comprehensive and more inclusive account of British history.

The value of this book will be evident to anyone who reads it, but I hope it will also stimulate greater interest in learning about the history of Liverpool's Black community and the context in which Ekarte did his work. This broader context helps us understand so much of what he did, why he did it, and the people that he worked with. The Liverpool 8 community in which he worked was the longest standing Black community in Great Britain. Black people had come from many parts of the world, and many were born there. A distinctive feature was the large proportion of African working class men, the majority of whom were seamen from West Africa working for Elder Dempster and other shipping lines.

Liverpool became like this because of its distinctive history. As a result of the slave trade and slavery the city saw the growth of a small but significant Black British population. Then after the British got out of the monstrous business of slavery and the slave trade, they massively expanded their intrusion into Africa. Liverpool was at the centre of the new trade, especially in West Africa, where the city controlled 80% or more. As many of the trading vessels' British crew died of diseases, African men were recruited to replace them. They were paid much less than the British seamen doing the same work and were worked harder – typically in the most difficult jobs in the fire room. On arrival in

Britain, the Africans were discharged and often abandoned, while white men were taken on. They settled, began relationships, and the mixed African and white population grew. Most of these families were segregated into one area, characterized by inferior housing, frequent joblessness and a poor economy. They were first segregated into Liverpool 1 around the docks (aka 'sailor town'), and then after the Second World War, they were relocated up the hill from Liverpool 1 to Liverpool 8, later known as Toxteth. The rest, as they say, is history. It's why Liverpool is so distinctive. And this is why so many of the people Ekarte helped were white, or mixed.

In other words, the 1950s Liverpool Black community was not the Windrush Generation of West Indian immigrants, most of whom married one another, had children and lived in several areas across Britain's major cities. Learning about these differences provides a broader picture of Black Britain.

Marika does not expect to be praised or receive establishment awards. But I strongly believe the book deserves an award. No one who reads it can fail to be indignant about British hypocrisy or outraged and saddened by the blatant racism that Ekarte faced at the hands of the British state and Britain's self-appointed moral leaders. Readers will also be inspired by Ekarte's dedication, determination, and stamina. Not only has Marika told his story, but she has also provided us with the foundations for finding out far more about his life, the work of the ACM, and the actions of many others with whom he was in contact. And she has paved the way for current and future generations to document the lives of men and women like Pastor Ekarte, that we may tell their stories too. A lot more needs to be found about him, and about the people he was supporting. Other people working on Ekarte will find this work invaluable.

Before I end, let me make a call to action. At the end of this book we are told that Pastor Daniels Ekarte was buried in an unmarked grave in Allerton Cemetery. That's a damn shame and it shouldn't be left like that. My brother Terry Small has recently identified the details of this plot and the information is at hand. People in Britain have been talking about removing or renaming statues and buildings and repatriating the stolen artefacts held in museums. How about creating a physical memorial or monument to Pastor Daniels? I've never heard of any recognition or commemoration of his grave to this date. And it would be a necessary and fitting corrective to the memorials in the city that champion the likes of William Gladstone in St. George's Gardens and Alfred Jones at the Pier head. Now wouldn't that be something?

Read this book and I guarantee that you will be moved. You will be inspired to read Marika's other works, because they too are full of information, insight and inspiration. I'm proud and honoured to call Marika a personal friend and a colleague. And I'm proud to write this preface to this new edition of her book. Pastor Daniels Ekarte has left us a legacy of self-determination, courage and endurance in the face of racist adversity, a legacy that should make us all proud. And we should be thankful to Marika. She has saved Pastor Daniels Ekarte's story from oblivion. We owe her a tremendous debt, and one of the best ways we can pay that debt is to expand her research.

Stephen Small
Oakland, March 2023

* * *

STEPHEN SMALL is a Professor in the Department of African Diaspora Studies at the University of California, Berkeley, where he has taught since 1995; and he is Director of the Institute for the Study of Societal Issues (which researches social justice and social change). He was born and raised in Liverpool 8, and has carried out research, with, about, and for Black people in Liverpool all his life. He has known Marika Sherwood since she first arrived in Liverpool and began research on Pastor Ekarte in 1992. He is currently writing a book on Black Culture in Liverpool in the 1970s-2000s, which will be published by Liverpool University Press in 2024.

Introduction

AT THE HEIGHT OF HIS ACTIVITIES PASTOR DANIELS Ekarte was a controversial figure in Liverpool. He challenged the 'establishment' in more ways than one, as I hope this book shows. As is the fate of many who assume a leadership role, especially among the dispossessed, or those who appear to be doing better than their neighbours, he was the subject of much criticism, both fair and malign. Today there are still disparaging rumours about him; for some of these I have attempted to give an explanation.

Researching Pastor Ekarte has been most enjoyable and rewarding, if at times very frustrating. His papers have disappeared. Liverpool police, which kept an eye on him and often harassed him, have destroyed their records. It is possible that there are wartime MI5 files on him, but such files are never made accessible to researchers. The Colonial Office, which from the 1940s had some responsibility for the Black population in the UK, has also destroyed most of its files. The present Bishop of Liverpool has informed me that there is nothing about the Mission in the Diocesan Registry.

Because of this paucity of information, the story is like Swiss cheese – as much substance as there are holes. Therefore this book can only be a beginning, a first, very imperfect attempt to restore Pastor Daniels to his place in the history of Liverpool and in the history of Black peoples in Britain. I hope others will expand and revise it and that in the not too distant future younger researchers will be telling me how much I had omitted and misunderstood and that the *real* story is ... In order to help these potential historians, I have given the full references to all the documents that I have found. This may be a little intrusive for those unfamiliar with such scholarly practice. Apologies: I hope you understand.

I must emphasise that this is not *a history of Liverpool's Black population, or even of the Black and White community in the Upper Hill Street area in the 1930s and 1940s. It is a mere outline of what one man, with the help of many neighbours and the women in the Mission, tried to accomplish.*

CHAPTER ONE

Liverpool 1860-1930

What was Liverpool like when the young Daniels Ekarte arrived there in about 1915, and when he established the African Churches Mission in 1931?

The social and economic background

In 1839, according to Oxford Professor Herman Merivale, Liverpool and Manchester owed their "opulence to the exchange of their produce with that raised by the American slaves...to the toil and suffering of the negro, as if his hands had excavated their docks and fabricated their steam engines".[1] Thus in the mid-nineteenth century Liverpool's prosperity depended as much on the products of slavery as its gigantic growth in the previous century had depended on the trade in enslaved Africans. Not that Liverpool had ceased being involved even in the evil merchandising of human beings: in 1862 Liverpool was still (and illegally) outfitting ships for the trade in slaves.[2]

Even with the ending of slavery in the USA in 1865, slavery in the Americas was not over: the last two countries to free their slaves were Cuba in 1880 and Brazil in 1888. Though Britain was supposedly staunchly against slavery, Britons invested heavily in these slave-worked countries; for example, in 1880 British investments in Brazil totalled £39 million, which was more than in any other country in South America; British exports totalled £6.9 million and imports £5.3 million.[3] In the latter half of the nineteenth century about half of the United Kingdom's exports and about one-third of its imports passed through Liverpool.

The international economic situation changed at the end of World War I. Britain's merchant fleets and factories faced tough competition from Germany and the USA. The seamen and dockers, who were over half of the employed male population of Liverpool, had always been poorly paid casual labour. Now they began to suffer longer and longer periods of unemployment. Local factories (mainly sugar and flour mills and oil seed crushing) did not provide enough jobs for the men – and very few for women, who were thus forced into domestic service. Unemployment increased rapidly; for example, in 1924 it was 21% among insured seamen; by 1932 the rate was 44%. Among all the insured workers of Merseyside unemployment was 28%, which meant that the total number of unemployed was in excess of 80,000. (Part-timers and casual labour were uninsured, as were 56% of seamen in 1932.)[4]

The conditions in which the poorest people in the city lived were abysmal. Frederick Engels, who visited Liverpool in the 1840s wrote that "a full one fifth of the population live in narrow, dark, damp, badly ventilated cellar dwellings... Besides these there are 2,270 courts, small spaces built up on all four sides and having but one entrance, a narrow, covered passage way, the whole ordinarily very dirty...". Conditions had not changed much by the end of the century: Dr E.W Hope, the Liverpool Medical Officer of Health reported in 1896 that in these "ceitar dwellings...families sleep in one inside room without light or ventilation". Some Liverpudlians had no more than one and a half square yards of living sleeping space.[5] In the 1930s, 42% of a sample of Liverpool families lived four or more to a 'house'; a family's home was often no more than a "room in an eighteenth century house, sub-let to a separate family, dilapidated and comfortless, lacking sanitary conveniences and even taps and sinks, nearly every family dependent for its cooking and heating of water on an incredibly unsuitable bedroom fire-grate".[6]

In a 1938 survey the Pilgrim Trust found that the standards of home management, family relations, domestic standards and state of furniture among Liverpool's unemployed was worse than in other areas of high unemployment in the UK; these low standards and the appalling housing conditions the Trust thought to be "to a large extent the consequence of unemployment", especially long-term unemployment, and Liverpool's unemployed "starting from a lower level when he falls out of work". Between 1930 and 1933 unemployment rose in Liverpool by 106% while in the rest of England and Wales it only rose by 76%. In 1933 about one in ten of the total population of Liverpool was in receipt of relief.

The city fathers can be held responsible for the creation of the dire living conditions as many of them owned such housing, and the Corporation was responsible for permission to erect and lease the 'court' and cellar dwellings. One writer on the economy of Liverpool has suggested that slaving must have had a degrading influence on the attitudes and philosophy of the town's commercial elite. The traders in slaves, a part of this elite, were also among the city fathers. For example, in the 1770s William Crosbie was merchant, slave trader and mayor. Much the same men owned the ships of the 19th and 20th centuries in which accommodation and provisions for sailors and seamen were as appalling as that which the men faced ashore. Not surprisingly, the same elite were held not to be very far-sighted in their provisions for employment training: in the 1930s the city was chided by the government for being "backward in regard to the provision of facilities for the training and instruction of able-bodied youngsters."[7] Or were these negligent 'fathers' perhaps only interested in a ready supply of cheap, unskilled labour for their ships, docks, warehouses and mills?

Between 1906 and 1930 Liverpool had considerably higher rates of infant mortality than the average for the UK. The city's Medical Officer blamed this on "ignorance and neglect on the part of the parents... The condition of the very squalid children begging in the streets, ragged and filthy, indicates the absence of any sense of parental responsibility"[8] The Liverpool Society for the Prevention of Cruelty to Children prosecuted hundreds of parents each year between 1891 and 1910 for neglecting their children. Dr E.W. Hope, the Medical Officer quoted above, who was so very ready to blame the parents and not poverty for the condition of children and excessive rates of infant mortality, was a vice-president of the LSPCC! (By way of a contrast to Dr Hope, the Medical Officers of Colne and Wigan listed poverty, filth, unsatisfactory systems for the disposal of sewerage, overcrowding, lack of clothing and home comforts as contributory causes of high rates of infant mortality.)[9] In 1934 the city's Public Assistance

Committee was forced to appoint a second – temporary – doctor to the Toxteth area when Dr J.J. Barry, then the sole doctor registering claimants for relief, complained that "the numbers of cases arising in the district are too great to cope with". (Claimants were registered and investigated by a Relieving Officer and a Medical Officer.) By the nineteenth century the Toxteth area contained 30% of the city's official paupers.[10] It was in Toxteth, in one of the city slums, that Daniels Ekarte set up the African Churches Mission.

Liverpool's population

The 1921 Census return showed that of a total population of 802,940 there were 6,861 Continental Europeans residing in Merseyside; the largest group among them were 3,393 "Russians, Poles, Finns, etc". It is probable that the majority of these were the Jews who had fled the Russian massacres of 1882. The next largest group in the Census was 6,054 from the "British Dominions, Colonies, etc". There were also 1,843 Americans, 678 "Latin" Americans, 571 Chinese, 107 Egyptians and 17 "Turks, etc".[11] A social survey conducted by the University found that 25% of the adult population had come to Liverpool from outside the area, many from Ireland.

There had been Africans or people of African descent living in Liverpool at least since the days of slavery in the eighteenth century, when a few enslaved Africans were sold in Liverpool; others had been brought to the area as the domestic servants of slaver captains, merchants and planters returning from the West Indian colonies. The status of slaves was not very clear in eighteenth and even nineteenth century Britain; certainly some of these slaves/servants were demanding wages as well as their freedom soon after arrival in the UK. However, having few skills other than those of domestic service, many found it difficult to obtain employment.

Other Africans must have come to Liverpool as seamen, ac whether in the British navy or merchant marine, or in the vessels of foreign traders. Others, free men and women, came from the colonies to seek a better life in Britain. They did not always find it readily; for example, a young man named John Hackett, the son of free parents in Jamaica, had been unemployed for so long that he had to ask for an advance on his wages to pay his debts when he was taken on as a servant to a Mr Cappe of Liverpool. We do not know how, why or when John Hackett came to Liverpool; he died in 1809, aged 25.[12]

After his visit to Liverpool in about 1860, Charles Dickens wrote of a pub's "negro" landlord; in the pub "the male dancers were all blacks". Henry Mayhew at about the same time noted that "many negroes are employed in Liverpool... They are hard working, patient and too often underpaid". Being underpaid was not the Black man's only problem: according to the police superintendent who accompanied Dickens around Liverpool, Blacks "generally kept together, because they are at a disadvantage singly and liable to slights in the neighbouring streets".[13] In 1847 the Foreigners' Mission in Liverpool reported working with Italians, French, Germans, and some "Heathens and Mohammedans".

As no-one has done any detailed research on the Black population in the nineteenth and early twentieth centuries, we do not know more about these Black men, or about the African woman who had a boarding house for Black seamen in the 1840s and '50s.[14] Were there other African women? How many? What about the population of mixed parentage, the descendants of earlier residents? The 1911 Census gives a breakdown of the population of the city by birthplace, but does not distinguish race, and so we do not know how many Liverpudlians were Black; how many of the 880 residents born in India were Indians, how many of the 495 born in Africa were Africans, or how many of the 198 born in the Caribbean were people of African descent. What is generally agreed upon is that during and after World War I the Black population increased considerably.

According to one researcher, Black people in the 1930s mainly lived in the "central and southern slums... They were confined to the poorest areas... The slum housing was, in many cases, over 100 years old and in a squalid condition". Dickens in 1860 had described these slums as a "labyrinth of dismal courts and blind alleys... the want of gaslight in the most dangerous and infamous of these places being quite unworthy of so spirited a town".[15] These sentiments of Dickens could have been applied to the 1930s; and almost to the 1990s, given the state of many of the areas I visited in my search for information on Pastor Ekarte.

Whites' attitudes to the Black population

The attitudes found by Dickens and Mayhew in the 1860s apparently existed 70 years earlier and as well as 70 years later. A Liverpool pamphlet of 1792, for example, called Africans "the most lascivious human beings".[16]

At the end of World War I many Black men who had shore jobs were dismissed – according to the *Liverpool Courier* some 120 lost their jobs by June 1919,[17] Many British African and West Indian seamen and soldiers demobilised in Liverpool at the end of the war could not find work. Some became so destitute that with the aid of the Liverpool Ethiopian Association they asked to be repatriated. Unemployment, poverty and racial tensions escalated. In May and June 1919 there were battles between Blacks and the police and numerous fracas in the streets which eventually grew into riots. Whites attacked Blacks, their homes and their hostels. They drove one Black man, Charles Wootton*, into the river. Pelted with stones, he drowned. The police did not arrest any of the lynchers. Nor did the media support the beleaguered Black community: the *Courier* in its editorial on the riots said "the average negro is nearer to the animal than is the average white man".[18]

There was apparently an attempt to enforce segregation in (certain premises by the early 1920s: the Wesleyan African Mission, started in 1923, had to use a separate entrance from the main mission, the "white and coloured congregation being, *by municipal order* quite distinct". (emphasis mine)[19]

Poverty deepened as the Depression took hold. Some even had to resort to the hated workhouse: the records of the Brownlow Hill workhouse register for surnames beginning with A-K for the six months July-December 1921 show that there had been 99 admissions of "colonials" – seamen, labourers, watchmen, dock workers as well as some wives and children. (The workhouse was the forerunner of today's "bed and breakfast hotels" for the homeless.)

The records of the various social agencies for the 1920s do not mention any Black peoples, but that does not necessarily mean that none received any help from them. It is possible that the agencies simply did not distinguish their clients by race. The Child Welfare Association's Annual Reports between 1940 and 1950 frequently printed the same photograph of children playing on the grass. One of the children is Black.

Besides this one photograph there is a little evidence of such involvement in the *Memoirs of the Liverpool Personal Service Society*, written in about 1931. The anonymous author mentions a White woman who about 14 years previously had been given a "half-caste baby to care for by the Guardians, and allowed 7/6 (37 ½p) a week in return". The woman was an invalid, unable to work at anything except "a little fancywork" (embroidery, I presume). The little girl's "father was superior in his own country. Her mother was a waitress after her father deserted this country and went back to his own. Once the father wrote offering the girl a good home in his country, but she would not leave the invalid who had been so good to her." Through the help of the LPSS worker this young woman became a piano teacher. "Of course, she does not charge as much as a white-skinned girl would." The author comments that the young woman had told her that at "school, when she was young, a few children skitted her colour and this had made her, in her own words, 'retire into her shell'".

A little later in her memoirs the author relates how a White woman married to a Black man had told her that it was "generally whites who first aggravated blacks, and she said that white women who betrayed their black husbands for a white man were never forgiven... 'It is not fair, it is bad enough for a white woman to deceive a white man, but it is hitting below the belt, missus, to marry a black man and to desert him for a white'"[20]

The racism of this social worker (in the use of the words 'of course') was very mild compared to that of the researcher in charge of the University's social survey of Merseyside. In 1934 D. Caradog Jones, Senior Lecturer in the School of Social Science at the University, which trained social workers, wrote that "Negro men not infrequently desert or die young and leave their 'wives and children dependent on Public Assistance... The settlement of Negro sailors... is a blot...on account of the serious results attendant on their intermarriage with white women."[21] That "negroes" might have wanted to return home at least partly because of the difficulty of getting jobs in Liverpool, or because, as Jones admitted, their wages were less than the White men's, does not appear to have influenced Jones' racist judgemental attitude. What the "serious" (and clearly undesirable) "results of intermarriage" were Jones did not bother to explain. The reader is obviously meant to understand and concur.

Jones was not the only one at the University imbued with racist attitudes. According to the warden of the University Settlement, by 1927 there had been "considerable unease for some time about something unspecified, which we are meant to understand to be Black/White marriages and the "resultant population of half-caste children". (Eugenicist academics and their followers believed that "racial purity was of utmost importance as racial "interbreeding" inevitably led to "mongrelisation"; these "mongrels" were deemed to be everything that the term implies, as well as inherently less intelligent than the "superior parent".) The School of Social Science invited a eugenicist researcher to address a meeting attended by, among others, head-teachers, the police, and Settlement staff. According to the Settlement's warden, Harold King, "the local vicar and two local headmasters substantiated Miss Fleming's evidence" to the effect that "in addition to the adverse factors in their heredity which often involved not only disharmony of physical traits but disharmony of mental characteristics, resulting in great strain, they had often no homes and were unable to obtain employment in any decent occupation". (It is not clear from the report if Ms Fleming believed that it was the "disharmony" that prevented people of mixed parentage getting decent jobs.)[22] As a result of this meeting an organisation called the Association for the Welfare of Half-Caste Children was established. The Association raised enough money to employ an ex-student of Liverpool University's School of Social Science,

Muriel Fletcher, to carry out a survey in Liverpool. Her *Report on an Investigation into the Colour Problem in Liverpool* was published by the Association in 1930, and created a lot of interest, according to the Association. Th*e Report* was circulated to Government departments, the police, social work and philanthropic organisations, MPs and the media.[23]

Fletcher's report is thoroughly biased as the sample of Black families she interviewed was drawn exclusively from people who had sought help from the various social service agencies in Liverpool. Written from a clearly eugenicist perspective, it was also scurrilously racist, and I will not dignify it by repeating its so-called findings. Her recommendations included the substitution of White seamen for Black, an official enquiry into the employment of "half-caste juveniles", and the appointment of a special "welfare worker as these families are influenced but little by the existing social organisations". To this racist attack Professor Roxby, the chairman of the Association, and head of the University's Geography Department, added that it "is clear that the present conditions under which coloured seamen from the West Coast of Africa enter Liverpool constitutes a real social menace... It would be a sin against posterity to allow a proved evil of this kind to remain unchecked." [24]

As if it wasn't enough for the Black population to have to contend with this sort of attack, it had been the pastor of the African Wesleyan Mission who had aided Ms Fletcher, to his subsequent chagrin. Mr Adkin was quick to take action to repudiate any responsibility on the part of the Mission for the report. Mr Ernest Adkin had been appointed to this Mission from its establishment in 1922/23; he held religious services and gave welfare advice and occasional small loans to Black peoples. He was in the Mission in Templar Hall, Mill Street, each morning from 10 till 11 "for consultation", and two evenings a week "when magazines and papers will be available".

Mr Adkin, a well-meaning paternalist, did not find his job easy. "The riots 2 or 3 years ago made them very bitter", he wrote to John Harris of the Anti-Slavery Society on 4 April 1923. "I feel that I have to win their confidence before I can do much with them. The ordinary attitude of English people to them is also a great hindrance to any work of the kind I am attempting." Mr Adkin was clearly shocked by some of the problems the men took to him. He took up some of these issues with government departments and informed Harris of his activities. For example, some seamen claiming reparations for property lost due to torpedo attacks during World War I had still not received any payments in 1923, four years after the war was over. One seaman's widow was still pleading for her pension. Mr Adkin wrote to John Harris in 1923 that he had not "heard of a single coloured man who has received any reparations though white men who were on the same ships have got their claim granted without difficulty". In another letter he wrote of former prisoners-of-war who had put in claims for compensation, but "each coloured man has been put off with some excuse". Equally distressing to Adkin were the reports reaching him that Elder Dempster (the employer of the majority of Liverpool's Black men) "had asked the Ministry of Labour and the Board of Guardians not to grant them (the unemployed Black men) any relief."[25]

Not surprisingly, the police joined in the attack on the Black population. Unfortunately Liverpool police have destroyed all their records and even the Home Office has not retained the special reports prepared on the "coloured people" in a number of British ports including Liverpool. However, some insight can be gained into the Liverpool police attitudes from a statement in the Watch Committee Reports for 1935. On page 23 the Report's section on Clubs states "one other club ... particularly revolting state of affairs ... frequented by white and coloured and half-caste men and women. Nightly scene of excessive drinking, foul language and filthy conduct, and dancing during which the grossest indecencies took place. Between and during the dancing indecent conduct between men and women was openly indulged in. The sanitary arrangements of this den were of the most primitive character." It seems inconceivable, in a port catering to large numbers of transient men from all corners of the world, that it was only in this club (the only one mentioned with a Black clientele) that conduct unacceptable to police eyes took place. According to Sierra

Leonean ex-seaman Ernest Marke, who had some experience of Liverpool and its police, "some members of the Liverpool Police had become so prejudiced against coloured men that their behaviour towards them had become nothing less than hooliganism".[26]

Did other city officials hold similar attitudes? Our only evidence is about the city's Immigration Officer and the Labour Bureau, The *Methodist Recorder* (29/5/1928) published a letter from the Mr Adkin in which he claimed that "a respected member of our Mission, born in a British colony", who had lived for 12 years in England and had a wife and child, was promptly deported when he became unemployed and went to sign on at the Labour Bureau. He was immediately imprisoned and put on board a ship on the same day. His wife and child were given 15 minutes before the boat sailed to say goodbye. The deportation was legal as the man could not prove he was a British subject, and by signing on had become legally destitute and thus liable for deportation as a destitute alien. However, Mr Adkin pointed out, this action by the Labour Bureau and the Immigration Officer left "the wife and her child dependent on the parish".

Was it such official actions that explain another aspect of what lay behind Jones' charge against Black men that they deserted their families?

The city's commercial sector was not immune to racist behaviour. George Schuyler, a well-known African-American writer, en route to Liberia in 1931, wrote of his experiences in Liverpool: when he arrived at the first-class Midland Hotel where he had made reservations, he was told that the hotel was full and was recommended to a second class hotel.[27]

What of the city's Whites living in the South End next door to Black families? One now elderly lady recalled of her young days in the 1930s, "prejudice was always in Liverpool, quietly. For instance if I or my sisters ever thought of marrying a Black man my father would have killed us. There were only certain types of women went with them. There were also many pubs in the South End which a White man would not enter, they were left strictly to the Black men and white women. So you see the prejudice was always there."[28]

The city's newspapers only carried news of Black peoples when they were in trouble with the police. The few other notices were almost invariably racist, at least until World War II. For example, the *Echo*, in its review of a book entitled *African Drums* on 11 October 1930 said "the healthiest race on earth is the Caucasian race, and the healthiest branch of that great race of the Anglo-Saxon". The *Daily Post*'s articles on the Richardson Report, whose findings formed the basis for the establishment of Port Welfare Committees, were as racist as the report itself. For example, on 8 July 1935 the paper wrote: "coloured men are not imbued with a moral code similar to our own... By marriage and with a family of children it is possible for them to live without work, and in receipt of more money than if they go to sea". On 9 July 1935: "In Liverpool the social changes consequent upon the influx of coloured men were giving rise to ever increasing anxiety among the authorities". In a letter printed on 11 July, Professor Roxby and Harold King of the Association for the Welfare of Half-Caste Children endorsed the Report, adding that these were "social questions of increasing urgency and difficulty".

International organisations, even those supposedly on the workers' side, were equally racist. The International Labour Organisation's report on UK ports, while admitting that there was less drunkenness (and a lower standard of living) among "coloured" resident seamen, noted "frequent irregular unions between coloured men and white women", as if such unions had been unknown among the White seamen. Clearly the problem was race, not irregularity. The report also quoted, without any criticism, the Liverpool Chief Constable as saying that "the problem of the coloured population has reached the stage which affects social conditions generally".[29]

The Black population

The resident population was of unknown size, originally mainly constituted of African men married to White women, and their children. The men found it almost impossible to obtain work on the docks or in the few local factories; from 1925 because of restrictive legislation and the racial discrimination advocated and practised by the National Union of Seamen, the men found it increasingly difficult even to obtain work on ships. Schuyler wrote that "there was absolutely no work for colored people, not even sweeping streets or the lowest domestic work". Though during the war work was more readily available, factory workers had to contend with the racism of their fellow workers.[30]

To the resident Black population must be added the transient African, African-American and West Indian seamen on British and foreign ships calling into or based at Liverpool. How long these men stayed in port depended on the availability of work, and their attachments – if any – to Liverpool. If the wait between jobs (and they were usually excluded from shore jobs) was long, these men became destitute. In 1932, when 0.7% of the registered unemployed in the city were "negroes". Caradog Jones reported that by 'tightening up the regulations with regard to the giving of benefit to unemployed negro seamen their inflow has been somewhat moderated".[31]

In 1938/39 a new survey found that about three-quarters of insured Black seamen were unemployed, 6% more Black than White families lived below the "poverty line", and that "coloured families" paid more for their accommodation than White families occupying the same number of rooms.[32] In April 1939 352 "Coloured" seamen were registered at the Employment Exchange; this was 4% of the total number signing on.[33] The position of young people was dismal: the Ministry of Labour admitted that the known unemployed (23 in 1936) was probably only a proportion of the true numbers. There was somewhat less of a problem in finding jobs for boys, at sea or as unskilled factory hands and shipyard workers, than in finding jobs for the girls. A number of boys were attending the Nautical Training School, with a promise of employment on completion of their course.[34]

Though even in this period a few became successful businessmen, most of the Black population lived in the ghetto of Toxteth (the South End), but this was a *ghetto of poverty*, not of race, as Black peoples lived side by side with the polyglot mixture of the city's poor.[35] They faced various levels of racist attitudes and racial discrimination at the hands of the police, the city's bureaucrats, the philanthropists, academics, clergymen, social workers, landlords and employers. One can now understand what experiences lay behind the accusation by the execrable Muriel Fletcher, that "they were influenced little by the existing social organisations".

NOTES AND REFERENCES

1. Herman Merivale, *Lectures on Colonization and the Colonies*, London, 1841-2, quoted in Cedric Robinson, *Black Marxism* (1983), Zed Press, 1992, p. 157. Merivale was appointed Professor of Political Science in 1837; he was Under-Secretary of State for the Colonies and then Under-Secretary for India, 1859.
2. British and Foreign Anti-Slavery Society, *Slave Traders in Liverpool – Extracts from Correspondence on the Slave Trade*, published by Command and Presented to Parliament, April 1862.
3. D.C.M. Platt, *Latin America and British Trade*, Adam & Charles Black, 1972, p.289; *Parliamentary Accounts & Papers* 1881, Vol.87; 1890-91, Vol.82. The £6.9 million to Brazil was 3.4% of total British exports; £5.3 million from Brazil was 1.7% of total imports. 12.6 million exports to Cuba in 1876 were 1.4% of the total; £2.9 million in imports was 1.0% of the total imports.
4. D. Caradog Jones, *Social Survey of Merseyside*, Vol.2, University of Liverpool, 1934, p.87.
5. F. Engels, *The Condition of the Working Class in England* (1845), Panther, 1969, pp.69–70. Report of Dr E.W. Hope, Liverpool Medical Office of Health, 1896, p.5. Data on living space from the excellent article by I.C. Taylor, 'The Court and Cellar Dwellings: the eighteenth century origin of the Liverpool slum', *Transactions of the Historic Society of Lancashire and Cheshire*, Vol. 122, 1970, p.86. **I am much indebted to Mike Boyle for sending me a copy of this invaluable article.**
In 1925, an ex-mayor of Bethnal Green, a very poor part of the East End of London, on a visit to Liverpool remarked that the houses around Marmaduke Street (on the edge of Toxteth) were only fit for demolition. *Liverpool Courier*, ?/9/1925.
6. Llewellyn Smith (ed), *The New Survey of London Life and Labour*, Vol. II, pp. 116-117, quoted in John Stevenson, *Social Conditions in Britain Between the Wars*, Penguin, 1977, p.202.
7. Stevenson, (see n.6), pp.269-279; D. Caradog Jones, *Social Survey of Merseyside: No. 9 – Public Assistance,* 1934, pp. 12–16. The suggestion that trading in slaves had a degrading effect on the city fathers was made by S.G. Checkland, 'Economic Attitudes in Liverpool 1793–1807', *Economic History Review*, 2nd Ser., Vol.5, 1952, pp.58-75, quoted in Taylor, (see n.5), p.80.

8. Report of Dr E.W. Hope, (see n.5), p.5.
9. LSPCC Annual Report, 1937. Stevenson, (see n.6), p.146.
10. Public Assistance Committee Minutes 11/6/1934. Ian G. Law, White Racism and Black Settlement in Liverpool, PhD Dissertation, University of Liverpool, 1985, p.50.
11. D. Caradog Jones, *Survey of Merseyside,* Vol.I, 1934, p.73.
12. *Memoirs of the Late Mrs Catherine Cappe*, London, 1826, pp.276–279.
13. Charles Dickens, *The Uncommercial Traveller (*1860), Oxford University Press, 1958, p.43; Henry Mayhew, *London Labour and London Poor*, Vol.4, 1862, p.229, quoted in Ian G, Law, (see n.10), p.71.
14. Law, (see n. 10), p.67.
15. Law, (see n.10), p.89; Dickens, (see n. 13), p.47.
16. *Fugitive Thoughts on the African Slave Trade,* Liverpool, 1792, quoted in Peter Fryer, *Staying Power*, Pluto Press, 1984, p. 165. This is another reference kindly sent to me by Mike Boyle. Liverpool attitudes were no less prejudiced towards the Irish, For example, at the Junior Empire Conference in 1937, Mr G.R.B. Simmons declared that the North was faced with a terrible influx of semi-civilised Southern Irishmen who come with the sole idea of qualifying for the dole". *Liverpool Daily Post*, 25/10/1937.
17. Law, (see n. 10), p.93.
18. Raymond H. Costello, British Attitudes to the Education of Black Peoples, M.Ed. Thesis, University of Liverpool, 1988, p.88; Fryer, (see n.16), p.300; and pp.299-302 for the Liverpool riots generally. The *Liverpool Courier* is quoted in Lord Gifford, Wally Brown & Ruth Bunday, *Loosen the Shackles*, Karia Press, 1989, p.29.
19. Ernest Adkin to John Harris of the Anti-Slavery Society, 3/1/1923, Rhodes House Library: Mss. Br. Emp. s.23, Box H1/3.
20. Merseyside Record Office: A Visitor, *Memoirs of the Liverpool Personal Service Society*, typescript, c.1931, pp. 150-2, 235.
21. Law, (see n. 10), p.98; D. Caradog Jones, S*ocial Survey of Merseyside,* Vol.II, 1934 p.102.
22. Constance & Harold King, *The Two Nations 1906-1937*, University Press of Liverpool, 1938, p.128. See also Paul B. Rich, *Race and Empire in British Politics,* Cambridge University Press, 2nd ed., 1990, pp.130-134.
23. Circular from the Association for the Welfare of Half-Caste Children, PRO:H045/25404/175483/9. I have been unable to find comments on Fletcher's report in the Liverpool newspapers, but this is probably due to an oversight.
24. M.E, Fletcher, *Report on an Investigation into the Colour Problem in Liverpool and Other Port*s, Liverpool Association for the Welfare of Coloured Children, 1930, p.6.
25. That Mr Adkin was anxious to repudiate the Fletcher report is in Liverpool Central Library: Wesleyan Minute Book, African and West Indian Mission Committee meeting 7/7/1930. This Minute Book was only recently found by Mr Peter S. Richards, the District Archivist of the Methodist Church. I owe thanks to Mr Richards both for searching out these records and for sending me photocopies. The Minutes, of only four meetings (June 1928-

July 1930), also contain the pamphlet issued by a committee set up to raise funds to refurbish and furnish the new mission building at the corner of Parliament and Great George Streets. The building was bought for the Mission with £1,600 donated by the Waddilove Trust. The pamphlet lists the members of the Committee: some were Wesleyans, the rest Liverpool worthies. Letters from Ernest Adkin to John Harris, January – July 1923, Rhodes House Library: Mss. Br. Emp. s.23, Box 41/3; the quotations are from letters n.d. (c.25/4/1923) and 15/5/1923 enclosing copies of Adkin's letters to the Under Secretary of State at the Colonial Office 5/5/1923. See also Paul B. Rich, 'Philanthropic Racism in Britain: The Liverpool University Settlement, the Anti-Slavery Society and the Issue of "Half-Caste" Children, 1919-1951', *Immigrants and Minorities*, 3/1, 1984, pp.69-8; Carlton E. Wilson, 'Racism and Private Assistance: The Support of West Indian and African Missions in Liverpool during the Interwar Years", *African Studies Review*, 35/2, 1992, pp.55-76.

26. Ernest Marke, *In Troubled Waters* (1975), Karia Press, 1986, p.51.

27. George S. Schuyler, *Black and Conservative*, Arlington House, 1966, p.177.

28. Interview with Mrs M. O'Brien, 18/6/1992.

29. International Labour Organisation (ILO), *Seamen's Welfare in Ports*, 1939, PRO: C0859/11/7. The Liverpool section of the report is based on a visit to the city 12-21 April 1939.

30. *Liverpool Daily Post*, 11/9/1942.

31. D. Caradog Jones, *Social Survey*, Vol. II, p.102.

32. D. Caradog Jones, *Coloured Families in Liverpool*, Liverpool University Press, 1940. This survey was sponsored by the Liverpool Association for the Welfare of Coloured People – the successor organisation to the one for the welfare of "half-caste children". Besides changing its name, probably under the influence of protests from many quarters, the Association had learned some lessons, despite Professor Roxby still being its chairperson. This survey, under the supervision of Caradog Jones, was carried out largely by Mr Hilton Prescod of British Guiana, a long-term resident of Liverpool. See also the works of Paul B. Rich cited in notes 22 and 24 above.

33. ILO Recommendations 1939, PRO:C0859/11/7.

34. Ministry of Labour to Col. J. Sandeman Allen MP, 16/12/1936, PRO: CO323/1521/2. The Liverpool Education Authority estimated that there was a total of 550 "negroid children aged under 18" in the city. Whether the Authority meant school-age children is not clear.

35. For the history of a successful Liverpool-born Black businessman, see Jeffrey Green, 'George William Christian (1872-1924): Liverpool Merchant', in Rainer Lotz and Ian Pegg (eds), *Under the Imperial Carpet*, Rabbit Press, 1986, pp. 69-77.

* There is disagreement as to the spelling of "Wootton".

CHAPTER TWO

Daniels Ekarte: Africa and the earliest years in Liverpool

Africa

According to his Identity Service Certificate, which was issued to colonial seamen in place of passports, George Daniel (the name Ekarte is not on the Certificate), was born in Calabar, Nigeria, on 1st January, 1904. This may of course not be accurate as Western-style bureaucracy in Nigeria was very elementary in those years and births were not recorded with officials. In 1926, the year the Certificate was issued, George Daniel was recorded as being five foot six inches tall, and of British nationality.

That he was issued with such a certificate did not necessarily mean that young Daniel was working as a seaman, though he had worked his way to Britain on a ship. In those days the British government was most reluctant to issue 'colonials' with passports, as these would have given them greater freedom of mobility. However, even the possession of this Certificate, clearly stating that he was British, gave the young man some security against deportation. In the 1920s and 1930s 'colonials' who could not prove that they were British and who were destitute (that is, applying for what was then called Public Assistance), could be deported. Many 'colonials' who settled in Britain did not have birth certificates and so could not prove that they were British. They thus found themselves classified as 'aliens' and faced deportation. Being classed as an 'alien' also meant that seafaring jobs were very hard to get, as Britons were employed first.

Why and when had George Daniel come to Liverpool?[1] According to the interviews he gave and what he had written about himself, many years ago he had worked as an errand-boy for Revd Wilkie, a Free Church of Scotland missionary in Calabar.

Another missionary, Mary Slessor, visited Dr Wilkie's mission station a number of times and the young boy was so greatly impressed by her that he left the service of Dr Wilkie and joined Miss Slessor in Itu. There he learned to "read my primers in English, to sing 'At the name of Jesus', and to say the Lord's Prayer in my native tongue". The young boy decided that he, too, would become a missionary. He began this work by "giving testimony at prayer meetings and by going to other villages to teach other children". Soon he became "fixed with a greater ambition, to go to the 'holy land' of England where my 'holy mother came from". Though Mary Slessor warned him that people in England were not "enthusiastic about heavenly things", he ignored these warnings and in 1915, after her death, shipped out as a galley-hand on an Elder Dempster ship.

This often repeated story of his early life makes it quite it clear that George Daniel could not have been born in 1904. Mary Slessor had died in 1915, so if the 1915 date is correct, he would only have been 11 years old when he landed in Britain. It is more likely that the impressionable and devout young man gave as his birth date the year that he went to the Itu mission. This could have been about 1904 as Mary Slessor had founded the mission in 1902, but it was not fully functional until 1904.

In 1905 Mary Slessor established a small mission, which she planned to be the first of many, at a village 5 miles from the town of Itu. She put in charge a boy of 12 named Etim, who read English well and who proved to be an able teacher. It is quite possible that George Daniel had been groomed to serve in a similar kind of capacity. This would mean that he had been born in the early 1890s.[2]

Arrival in Liverpool

If the date of his arrival had indeed been 1915, as given in the interviews, it is curious that Mr Ekarte never mentioned World War I or the 1919 anti-Black riots. Is it possible that he was mistaken in the date, or wished to falsify it for some reason? There seems to be no way to clear up this mystery.

The young man was shocked by Liverpool: by the cheeky children, the quarrelling, swearing, racism and general licentiousness compared to Itu. He worked for a while at Bibby's oil mills and at Fairrie's sugar refinery. But times were hard and Ekarte drifted into gambling and became "a partner in some vicious occupations". He bought a gun, determined to return to Calabar and "shoot all missionaries, black and white" because they had deceived him. He also intended showing the "various chiefs my note book in which I had written down all the insults I had received from the 'Christian people in the 'holy country'".[3]

Fate intervened. One Sunday morning he was walking past 4 Hardy Street, where Africans, used to meet to worship. He usually avoided this place, but on this day he heard a voice calling him and he went in. "A great light came into my heart. I went in and knelt down to pray." Soon afterwards Ekarte threw his gun and notebook in the Mersey and began a new life. The year was 1922.

This dramatic account of his early years in Liverpool comes from Daniel Ekarte's own testimony over the years. Is it all true? There is no way of knowing. As all these accounts appeared in missionary magazines, his own publications, or in popular magazines at times when he was desperately trying to raise funds for his Mission, it is possible that Ekarte might have embellished the facts. But a kernel of truth is probably there.

Missionary in Liverpool 1922–1932

Daniels Ekarte now began "holding services in private rooms and in the open air... All sorts of people listening, Chinese, Arabs, Africans like myself". An African man preaching in the street was not a welcome sight to the police, especially one attracting a crowd. Ekarte was arrested twice on charges of obstruction. Refusing to pay the fine, he was jailed. In jail he continued to preach and sing hymns. He also claims that once he was sent to the mental hospital on Brownlow Hill to have his sanity investigated; but there was no hospital there, only a workhouse for the destitute. He was declared sane. Besides preaching in the street, Ekarte began visiting Africans on ships, in lodging houses and hospitals.

From this point onwards what we know of Daniels Ekarte's early life is based on what I learned from Mrs A. Ankrah, whose father and husband were both involved with the preacher, For unknown reasons Ekarte had to stop preaching at 4 Hardy Street, where there was a Coloured Men's Religious Institute run by a Pastor William Bernard. He then preached at the Gospel Hall on the corner of Dickenson and Pitt Streets.[4] When he had to leave there also, he was offered space for religious services by the Aditunje family from Ghana at 16 Cookson Street. He was married then, to a White woman named Lily; they had a son named George. Mrs Ankrah, then a child herself, remembers George playing in their backyard.[5] Lily died in about 1927 and young George was fostered by Mrs Hannan, whose husband was a cabinet maker, at 25 Almond Street. With financial aid from an increasing number of supporters, Daniels Ekarte hired a hall in Dickenson Street, but, Mrs Ankrah recalls, he was hounded out of there by racist hooligans.

NOTES AND REFERENCES

1. The early life story given here is compiled from an early auto biography and various interviews and newspaper articles, e.g. Daniels Ekarte, 'My Conversion' and 'My Bitter Disappointment', African Churches Mission pamphlet, Rhodes House Library: Anti-Slavery Society Papers, Br. Emp. Mss. s.23, Box H1/2 1; Revd | Chalmers Lyon, 'A Footnote to the Life of Mary Slessor', *The Life of Faith*, 1/1/1932, pp.565-6; 'African Churches Mission in Liverpool', *Liverpool Diocesan Review*, Vol. 6, 1931, pp.328-330; Gilbert Adams, 'African Churches Mission and Training Home', *African Torchlight,* Issue 1, Winter 1953; articles which focus on other issues related to the Mission, and which are cited later, usually contain elements of the same story.

2. Information on Mary Slessor from W.P. Livingstone, *Mary Slessor of Calabar*, Hodder & Stoughton, London, 1917. Cheryl McEwan, a current biographer of Mary Slessor whose PhD is not yet complete, kindly searched her materials for me but could find no trace of George Daniel or a George Daniels Ekarte.

3. This account is also unverifiable. Police records have been destroyed and it has not been possible to trace a mental hospital in the vicinity. Brownlow workhouse records exist, but without an admission date, the task of finding a name would take months of work.

4. There was another mission in the area, the Methodist African and West Indian Mission Religious and Social Institute, at 73 Parliament Street, which "was taken in 1928 and used mainly for social work through preaching

services were held. The latter were not continued after 1948." Ian Sellers, *The Methodist Chapels and Preaching Places of Liverpool and District, 1750-1951*. **I am most grateful to Mr Peter S. Richards of Wallasey for sending me this information.**

5. A search of the Register of Marriages for this period did not reveal a record for George Daniels Ekarte; similarly there is no record of the birth of a George Daniels or a George Ekarte during the years 1921-1927; neither is there a record of the death of Lily Ekarte or Lily Daniels between 1927 and 1931.

CHAPTER THREE

The African Churches Mission Opening, July, 1931

Once he had returned to Christ and had established a following, Daniels Ekarte set about raising funds to set up a permanent mission home. (Was the change in name also symbolic?)

In July 1930 the Church of Scotland Foreign Missions Committee, who had originally sponsored Mary Slessor, considered a plea for financial assistance from Daniels Ekarte. The Committee noted that "four or five friends" had investigated and reported favourably on his work in Liverpool. Dr Wilkie, the young George Daniel's employer in Calabar many years previously, was asked to bring the matter of supporting this work before the Gold Coast Mission Council, where he was now in charge. The Calabar Council was also asked to consider aid. Dr Wilkie's brother, a businessman recently ordained a minister at Hoylake, was also contacted. As Ekarte had said that he would be delighted to "have a committee behind him if you [Mr Wilkie) were on that committee"; would he undertake to form such a committee?[1]

Unfortunately as many of the records of the Foreign Missions Committee have been lost, we do not know exactly what happened. However, the announcement of the opening of the African Churches Mission in the *Liverpool Diocesan Review* stated that the Trustees were Canon A.L.J. Shields (Vicar of St. Catherine's, Abercromby Square, Liverpool), Revd J.W. Wilkie and P. Howarth Esq of Grove Street, Liverpool. The Mission's president was the Bishop of Liverpool.

Revd Shields presided over the opening ceremonies on 7 July 1931, which were attended by a "crowded company of devout coloured men" and the Trustees. The opening itself was performed by the Bishop. Daniels Ekarte was now officially the pastor of the African Churches Mission.[2]

The Mission consisted of two "knocked together" houses at 122-124 Hill Street, Toxteth, Liverpool 8. Through an anonymous donation and with help from the Church of Scotland, Pastor Ekarte had signed a three-year lease on the buildings. The furnishings were clearly sparse as the Revd Shields appealed for furniture and furnishings, papers and books for the reading room, and hymn books for services, as well as for volunteer teachers.

Was it the African Churches Mission that George Schuyler visited in 1931? He wrote that he had been to a "mission serving coloured people. Most of them were sailors and almost all were married to English women. These white wives fought to get a square deal and equal rights for their husbands, but it was tough going."[3]

But, however spartan, Pastor Daniels' accomplishment in obtaining so much support and setting up his Mission in the midst of an economic depression is most impressive. He was an untrained man, with limited mission education, who had arrived in Liverpool penniless. He had no claims on any particular denomination, nor had he friends in high places. The level of support he obtained in a society where even clergymen were not immune from holding racist beliefs and where class-divisions were rife, is testimony to the Pastor's character and quality of work.

The *Liverpool Daily Post* reporter who attended a service at the Mission about a year after the opening left us this description: "a congregation of about eighty crowded into a simply furnished room, with a picture of Christ above a blue cloth-covered dais – a print of Durer's *Praying Hands* on the yellow-distempered wall... Several white people among the Africans... A choir of eighteen, all in cassocks and surplices... The mission is undenominational but the service followed Church of England lines... Hymns were sung with extraordinary fervour to the accompaniment of a harmonium played by one of the three red-cassocked precentors. The whole service had an almost revivalist enthusiasm... Few of the congregation could afford more than a copper (for the collection)... The mission depends on donations and occasionally receives help from Africa."[4]

By 1938 the Mission, involved in a multitude of activities, was still anything but luxurious. Ethel Fegan of Girton College, Cambridge, a member of the Save the Children Fund, visited the Mission. She described it as having "on the ground floor, Pastor Ekarte's office, a small billiard-room, and a kind of snack-bar for simple meals, and in a tiny yard at the back he tries to run a Brownie pack. Upstairs, the first floor front rooms of the two houses have been made into one to form a chapel, furnished with chairs, harmonium and reading desk. At the back is a room where girls and women can do sewing and on the top floor are two tiny flats, one his own living quarters and the other for visitors. The whole house is scantily furnished, with the very barest minimum necessities, but his evident pride and joy in it and its obvious poverty brought tears to one's eyes. "[5]

What sort of area was Hill Street? It is difficult to picture it now as redevelopment has destroyed not only the old streets but also their history. Hill Street was quite a long street, ending up at the docks on the Mersey. The Mission was quite some way from the Mersey, on the corner of Hyslop Street. This was a short street which, in 1935, held the Tontine vaults, St. Patrick's Roman Catholic School, the Presbyterian Mission Room, a marine stores dealer and a shop owned by Mrs Colenso. On Hill Street, next door to the Mission were two companies manufacturing mineral water; then came two midwives, a tobacconist and a wardrobe dealer (used clothes). Opposite was a cooper's, Thos. Dodd & Co, a pub and William Shiells, a large pawnbroker. There were altogether three pubs in the street, and innumerable small shops such as confectioners, grocers, fish mongers. Many of the names listed in Gore's Directory sound Irish and it seems that the docks-end of the street housed mainly dock workers.

Clearly a multi-racial, multi-ethnic and multi-faith area, sheltering many seamen and dockers and their families, crowded among small factories, second-hand stores, warehouses and the inevitable pubs and pawnbroker.

NOTES AND REFERENCES

1. Library of Scotland, Edinburgh: Church of Scotland Foreign Missions Committee, Minute Book for 15/7/1930, Dep.298/158; letter to Revd J.W. Wilkie 30/7/1930, Home Letter Books of the Secretaries of the Foreign Missions Committee, MS.7733. In response to my request, Professor Paul Dukes of the University of Aberdeen requested the University's Archivist to search the Free Church materials in the University's collections. Sadly Colin McLaren found nothing pertaining to Pastor Daniels. (Letter from C. McLaren, Head of Special Collections, University of Aberdeen, 26/10/ 1993. **I wish to thank both Professor Dukes and Mr McLaren for their help. Requests for information to Edinburgh institutions elicited no response**.

2. *Liverpool Daily Post*, 8/7/1931

3. Schuyler (see n.26, ch. 1), p. 178.

4. *Liverpool Daily Post*, 21/10/1932.

5. *The World's Children*, January 1938; Ethel Fegan, 'West African Girls in England', manuscript, n.d., Girton College, Cambridge: Ethel Fegan Papers. **I am grateful to the College's Archivist, Ms Kate Perry, for sending me photocopies of excerpts from these Papers.**

CHAPTER FOUR

The Mission's work, 1930-1945

Daniels Ekarte became known as Pastor Daniels, and to some youngsters as Daddy Daniels. Some of my White informants wrote me that he had also been known as 'Nigger Dan', but assured me that no disrespect was implied. (It is difficult to believe that even sixty years ago Whites were not aware of the racist insult.) In the 1930s and 1940s Pastor Daniels was a popular and respected figure in the Hill Street community, both Black and White. His concerns and hence his work were as rooted in the practical as the spiritual.

Activities at the Mission

In 1934, 380 men and 86 women were 'registered' with the Mission and 148 children were on the Sunday School list. The average attendance at the Sunday morning and evening services was 62, and at Sunday School, 42. By 1936 membership had risen to 558. Some parents, members of other congregations, sent their children to the Pastor's Sunday School because of the free (or cheap) breakfasts they could have there. There were also daily services, prayer and gospel meetings and overnight services. Mrs Rita Reeves remembers the services being "packed – people used to stand outside. There was a proper hymn, and gospel singing." For a while the Pastor also led a hymn-singing group around the local streets in the early morning, but he was soon asked by those trying to get some sleep to stop this.

For the children, there was also scouting: when the Scout Troop was registered in 1934, there were 18 members, led by Frank Bailey and Thomas Bassey. The Troop, the 348th Liverpool, known as the Liverpool Africans, grew to 28 by the late 1930s. It was officially disbanded on 3rd October 1945, though it is still listed in a slightly later report of the Mission, with a Mrs Adam as its scoutmaster.[1] There were 31 girl guides and a Brownie pack, led in the mid-1940s by Mrs Roberts.

There were also music and secondary school classes, with 53 pupils. Pastor Daniels was always concerned with the education of Black children, especially as in the 1930s there were hardly any Black children getting into secondary or technical schools. (Secondary schools were only for the academically successful or the wealthy as children had to pass a series of highly competitive examinations for the few scholarships available. Even with a scholarship, parents had to pay for books and uniforms. One Black girl in Manchester who had won a scholarship was not granted it because the headteacher assumed that her parents could not pay the additional costs. Another Black girl, in Liverpool, was not allowed to sit the examination because she had often been late to school. Her headteacher was not interested in her excuse, that her mother having died, she had to get all her young brothers and sisters ready for school. Further research would probably reveal more instances of such behaviour by head and class teachers.)[2]

There was a Mother's Union, which sometimes went on excursions. The Mission had a reading room supplied with newspapers where the men also played dominoes, and a billiard room.

But that was not all. According to the report for 1933, some 13,336 free meals had been given to the poor", of whom there were many, both Black and White, in Depression-ravaged Liverpool. In 1936, 3,040 free breakfasts had been served to children and 3,444 free meals to adults. "Daniel Ekarte stood by the door every morning asking children on their way to St. Patrick's school if they had had their breakfasts. If not, he gave them toast and a drink", said 80-year old Mrs O'Brien, Mr Nathaniel Laryea, then a seaman from the Gold Coast, remembers the two missions in the district, but Pastor Daniels' was more popular "because we could go there to eat breakfast, lunch and dinner".

In an emergency homeless men were given a bed; meals were available for a small fee or free to those who could not pay for them. Most often the homeless were referred to rented rooms for which the Mission paid until the man found work or some means of support.

At Christmas Pastor Daniels always organised a large party for anything up to 200 children. He sought special funds and local firms and shops gave food and toys for the children. A local shop, Yaffe's sweet shop, owned by Joe and Mary Brennan, used to give sweets to the children, according to Mr Dave Young. There was also a Christmas party for all the Mission members. [No information has come to light about the source of the special funds. In 1944 the Merseyside Council for Hospitality gave the Mission three guineas *(£3.15)* towards the Christmas party. It is not known if this was a regular donation. By 1943, if not earlier, the Colonial Office also gave a donation and Major Taafel, the US Army Chaplain in the area, provided chocolates and toys.[3]]

The Mission became the local centre for those in need. Wives and children fleeing abusive husbands would be sheltered. Mr McKavitt, as a child, used to deliver groceries to the Mission from the shop across the street and recalls that its owner thought the world of Pastor Daniels. (This was probably Hamilton's grocery.) "There was a basement in the Mission and Pastor Daniels used to give us buns and tea and talk to us and tell us all sorts of things." Mr Dave Young, who as a youngster used to live and work nearby, remembers the Mission in the late 1940s as being an "open house, the door never shut, anyone was welcomed, colour of skin made no difference... I am white, but sometimes when I was going home from work, I would pass his place and he would wave me over and say "You look tired. He would give me a cup of tea and a fag and put his arm around me, and ask me all about my work... He would sit on the steps in the summer, and talk to all who passed by. He wasn't a big man; he had white curly hair and a close white beard. He was liked by all the local people and he was very well known and respected."

Mr Laryea concurs that Pastor Daniels "had no ill feeling for anybody. He was a nice gentleman. He always wore a robe with a large cross on his neck, a small hat (cap) and rosary beads in his hand. He had a very beautiful face and was very quiet."

During the war, when the Pastor was an Air Raids Precautions warden, bombed-out families were given floor-space in the Mission until they were re-housed. In about 1940 "one night an ammunitions ship blew up", Mr Rogers remembers. "A lot of people sheltering in the Mission cellar jumped out of their skins. The building shook...the tiles of the roof came down and the windows crashed in. Next morning, there was Pastor Daniels, sleeves rolled up, helping out with the cleaning up and giving words of comfort."

The one surviving Ledger kept by the Pastor reveals the very wide range of people and kinds of help offered at the Mission.[4] The Ledger begins in December 1930, with a list of stowaways who had been provided with money for rent and for food for a week; they were sometimes helped to find work on board ships. By April 1931 the entries include solicitors' fees, doctors and hospitals' bills, aid to the sick, including children, and financial aid for families and single men.

The level of poverty in the area is indicated by the number of entries for money for boots, for winter coats and for burials. For example, "Mr and Mrs J., rent, as they were going to be put out by the landlord, £1/15/0" (£1.75); "T.J., help when he came out of prison, ten shillings". In January 1933 the Mission gave Miss U.A., a schoolgirl, a "typewriting fee", presumably for lessons; she had also received five shillings (25p) for a pair of boots the previous November.

One entry indicates how difficult the police could make life for those who tried to help themselves. In September 1933 "Mr Johnson, a poor man who always earn his living by means of going about with his instrument of music, was arrested, and was bound over for 12 months. Any further play by him in any corner of the street or Public Houses during which period, he shall be fined £5." Mr Johnson was given five shillings to "help his daughter who is in Hospital in confinement".

There are no entries from October 1933 to May 1934. From June the entries are for people who needed a solicitor. One of these, entered on 17 August 1934, gives us another glimpse of the relationship between the Black population and at least some city policemen. As Mr James Isaiah was just about to enter the Unemployment Office to 'sign on', a policeman stopped him and would not let him enter even when Mr Isaiah produced his signing-on card. The policeman allegedly said "If you don't get away, I'll show you, you have no right to be signing on the dole". Mr Isaiah was arrested and charged with obstruction. The magistrate fined him ten shillings. As it is hardly conceivable that a White man would be prevented from signing-on, we are entitled to presume that Mr Isaiah was Black.

There are no entries at all for 1935, only one for 1936, and none for 1937. Had it proved impossible for the Pastor to raise the funds to continue providing much needed services, or did he not receive enough clerical help to be able to maintain the ledgers? Between 1938 and 1944 the entries are irregular. They are mainly lists and depositions of stowaways as well as a few briefer entries, such as expenses for a baby who had been run over by a motor car, an excursion by the Mothers' Union, and a funeral ceremony at the Mission. The majority of the stowaways were from Sierra Leone and Nigeria, with quite a few from the then British West Indies.

Not all these people made their own way to the Mission, though it was well-known among seafarers. Many were referred by other agencies. The first explicit referral from the police is for someone listed only as Yatarrah, "found drifted" in January 1933 and again two months later. The first actual mention of the Immigration Office referring a stowaway to the Mission is entry number 25, John Williams, in August 1932. In 1937 Pastor Daniels told Ethel Fegan (mentioned in chapter 2) that "he is now called in to help by the Liverpool police. When any black seaman gets into trouble, and any who have nowhere to go are directed to him".[5]

In 1934 the city fathers were alarmed at the alleged increase in the number of West Africans being smuggled into the country. The Police Criminal Investigation Department was asked to look into the possible involvement of African crews and some kind of connivance on the Gold Coast (now Ghana). What became of this investigation is not known, but certainly African seamen were dragged into the courts on charges of aiding and abetting stowaways. One such man was Reginald Ankrah, who, with his shipmate George Nelson, was charged with "aiding and abetting" Charles Hanson, aged 18, to stow away on a Swedish ship. Ankrah was discharged, Nelson fined £4 and Hanson was imprisoned for 14 days. On his release Hanson was taken to the Mission by the "Police Missionary".[6] Mr Ankrah was already known to Pastor Daniels as in August 1932, when he had been without work for some months, he had applied to the Pastor for help. He later became choir-master at the Mission, where he also played the organ. Reginald Ankrah was one of "two sensible men" aiding the Pastor, according to Mr Laryea. The other was Edwin DuPlan, also from the Gold Coast.

Not all those aided by the Mission were locals or even seamen searching for work all over the UK. Occasionally African and Indian students were taken in. Mrs Reeves recalls "turbaned" Indian students staying for six months or so because they could not get lodgings elsewhere. The Ledger records three students, one of whom turned out to be a fraud: Moreton had been given "shelter and food and was here with us for six months after which period we found out his story weren't truth with that & etc he went away un-noticeable, but he is in town". This scoundrel had cost the Mission £12. In 1938 Nigerian student Nwafor Orizu en route to Lincoln University in the USA, stayed at the Mission. He had been recommended by Nnamdi Azikiwe, who had known Pastor Daniels "well".[7]

The Mission also received referrals from other charitable organisations. Entry number 65 is for Cecil Hunte, of British Guiana, who had travelled from London to Manchester and from there to Liverpool searching for work. Not finding any, he sought help from the African and West Indian Mission, but all the Revd Lawson did was give him a note to Pastor Daniels. Another applicant referred to the Pastor by Mr Lawson in September 1938 was "a Paddy boy". Pastor Daniels sent him to "St. Patrick's Priest round the corner and he refused to help the poor boy and the boy returned to us. We gave him something to eat and a few shillings to pay his way. Wishing God's blessing. He is 18, from Dublin." According to an entry for 22 July 1939, even the Mayor's office referred poor applicants to the Mission.

The early entries seldom indicate the recipients' nationalities: one exception is a German, and another, an entry for a "whiteman". As many Africans and West Indians have 'English' names, one can draw no conclusions from family-names. Neither can we draw any from the very lack of nationalities as the entries are in many hands and vary so much in style and content that we cannot assume that the absence of nationality indicates recipients of African descent.

The Mission's Helpers

Some of the neighbouring women came to help and a Mrs Carruthers did some secretarial work and book-keeping for a time. The numerous different scripts in the Mission's Ledger and in the handwritten letters signed by Pastor Daniels indicate a variety of helpers with different levels of skills.

Obviously Pastor Daniels needed help with the cooking and housekeeping at the Mission. Soon after the Mission opened he found a housekeeper, a Mrs Roberts (also known as Mrs Morris), a mother of four who had run away from her husband. By the terms of the divorce settlement the four girls were split between their father and maternal grandmother. However, the grandmother became ill and the twin girls she had been caring for were put into care. Hearing this Pastor Daniels insisted that the twins move to the Mission. The two girls virtually became part of the Mission's housekeeping staff. At their mother's insistence, before school they took breakfast trays to anyone staying in the Visitor's Room, laid the dining room table, helped cook breakfast and did some cleaning. After school there was more cooking to be done. They also helped clean the whole house "from top to bottom", including the cellars; the bare wood floors were scrubbed and even the railings in the front of the building had to be washed. They also helped with the washing. The twins Rita and Rose, now Mrs Reeves and Mrs Phillips say of their mother that "she was hard", but speak of Pastor Daniels with the greatest affection: "he was like a dad to us", they recall. James Phillips remembers that as children he and his family used to visit Pastor Daniels every Sunday and call him 'grand-dad'.

But the Pastor was not a saint, as some speak of him. Some people remember him as unsympathetic and arrogant, and elitist towards the less educated. (As the Pastor himself had little formal education, and some thought needed help with "the scriptures", this 'elitism' may in fact have been a shying away from the better educated.) Nevertheless, even some of his critics attended services and other functions at the Mission.

The Pastor fell foul of some segments of the Black community when a personal relationship developed between himself and Mrs Roberts around 1938–39. The Calabar men, who used to meet "in council" to sort out minor disputes and problems, attempted to convince Pastor Daniels of the error of his ways. The Pastor would not listen and the men decided to withdraw their support from the Mission. Though undoubtedly attendance at Mission services declined for a while, it rebounded somewhat in the early 1940s. Despite this aspect of his history being common knowledge, Pastor Daniels was again used by Nigerians, maybe especially those newly arrived, as a source of help. "He was a good man. Always stood by people in trouble", thought Mr Johnson, who had arrived in 1940.[8]

Activities Outside the Mission Walls

Pastor Daniels visited the poor and the needy in their homes, in hospital and in police cells. For example, the Mission's report for 1936 (one of the very few to survive) lists 427 hospital visits and 4,213 house calls as well as 430 visits to ships. The cost of these, more in terms of energy than his bus fares, must have been prodigious.

Other Activities

In its 7 March 1934 issue the *Liverpool Daily Post* printed a letter from an anonymous 'Houseowner' asking "who is responsible for the continued influx of negro men, women and children... The trouble...black and white living together gets more noticeable and intolerable." The writer pleaded for someone to help "those who are trying to keep a once select neighbourhood (the South End) still select". This letter led to a spirited correspondence between Pastor Daniels and a number of anonymous, racist letter-writers. The Pastor replied the next day that "coloured people's behaviour does not call for any serious criticism". In another letter he wrote that there was no law against inter-racial marriages. Why do the complainants have a problem with Negroes coming to Britain when "Englishmen go to Africa, driving Negroes into the backlands", he asked. Liverpool's Negroes neither held orgies "nor do they figure disproportionately in the courts. Negroes are looking forward to see what place politically they will attain as Britishers – therefore we are expecting British justice free of prejudice". (12/3/1934) To further diatribes against "orgies of singing and dancing...black men and white women", the Pastor responded by pointing out that "the law is there to prevent any indecent behaviour in dancing halls, which behaviour is not peculiar to negroes alone". The editor gave the final word to 'Adsum', before declaring the correspondence closed. 'Adsum' wrote that "the apparent influx of negroes cannot prove anything but deleterious", a situation which "could easily become a menace". (16/3/1934)

To be fair, it must be mentioned that a J.M. Style, in a letter published on 13 March, had written that "some of us feel ashamed that the few honest negro workers who have come to our city should be treated with so little courtesy. We cannot forget that the white race holds a large part of Africa and that Liverpool has not been guiltless in her treatment of the black race."[9]

One has to ask a question about what was going on beneath the surface regarding Black peoples in Liverpool in 1934; a question to which I can only provide a hypothesis for an answer. Why was it in that year that the weekly journal *West Africa*, which rarely mentioned Black people (except students) in the UK, raised the issue of the alleged increase in stowaways?[10] What led to the alleged concern by the city fathers? What led to the anonymous correspondents complaining about Black neighbours and the presence of Black peoples? Who was the Frank Crosby who wrote from the Catholic Club in Southampton to Dr W.J. O'Donovan, MP, regarding "coloured seamen in Liverpool living off young girls?[11] There were no external events of significance. Is it possible that some of the activities of Pastor Ekarte, especially those related to fighting for Black people's rights in the courts, with the police and with employers was displeasing the authorities? Or had the tabloids created a scandal which researchers have not yet discovered?

A number of people mentioned that Pastor Daniels was often harassed by the police, but without police records, we have no evidence. Even if he was subject to such treatment, it did not deter him from the struggles of the day, whether local or international.

The first evidence of the Pastor's overtly political activities is in the Jamaican *Daily Gleaner* of 8 August 1934, which reported that he had been one of the speakers on "Negroes in Africa' at the conference on "The Negro in the World'. Pastor Daniels was in distinguished company: among the other speakers were the Hon. K.A. Korsah (member of the Gold Coast Legislative Council; Otto Huiswoud, editor of the Negro Worker, Arnold Ward, secretary of the Negro Welfare Association; Jomo Kenyatta of the Kikuyu Central Association; Harold Moody, president of the League of Coloured People and Harry O'Connell, a communist seamen's organiser in Cardiff.[12] The conference was thus an opportunity for Pastor Daniels to meet activists of various political faiths and to make contact with those he had not met before.

In the same month, at special services held to commemorate the emancipation of slaves, Pastor Daniels declared that "his people had suffered terribly from the greed, lust, viciousness and injustice of those who had imposed on them the horrors of slavery", according to the brief account in the *Daily Post*. In 1935 during the Remembrance Day Services, there was a special meeting addressed by Edwin DuPlan, described as a journalist. The meeting passed a resolution: "We, Africans in Liverpool, appeal to His Majesty's Government to exercise its power to maintain peace in Abyssinia". (Abyssinia, then one of the two free countries in Africa, was being threatened by an Italian invasion.) DuPlan was to formulate a petition to be sent to the King, with a copy to the local MP, J. Gibbins. Whether the petition was sent to the King is not known; the Colonial Office received it in June 1936.[13]

In 1936 the Remembrance Day Services in October were addressed by two speakers: the Marxist anti-imperialist George Padmore and by George Smith of the Aborigines Rights Protection Society, a Gold Coast nationalist organisation.[14]

In his 1938 brochure Pastor Daniels listed among the Mission's aims "To endeavour to obtain reasonable hours of duty and fair wages for seafaring workers, and to use every legitimate effort to provide for their safety". This was bound to put him on a collision course with the authorities and the city's shipping companies. However, as the government kept activist Black people under surveillance, Pastor Daniels must already have been seen as a potentially dangerous character because of his association with radicals such as Huiswoud, Ward, O'Connell and Padmore.

[From 1911 onwards there was collusion between the Seamen's Union, the British government, the National Maritime Board (which fixed seamen's wages and conditions of work) and certain shipping companies about unequal pay for seamen recruited from the colonies. In some cases this agreement to discriminate was extended to 'colonial' seamen resident in Britain. One of the many shipping companies party to this collusion was Elder Dempster, which for many years held a near-monopoly on shipping to West Africa. Elder Dempster owned innumerable subsidiaries – many in West Africa. In the mid-1930s the company was taken over by Alfred Holt & Co, the Blue Funnel Line.] [15]

Pastor Ekarte's 1938 aim of fair wages was a direct challenge to Elder Dempster, a commercial power in Liverpool, many of whose directors held important civic posts in the city. This iniquitous, (anti-union in West Africa) company had a 4-tier wage system in 1940: at the lowest rate were 'raw recruits from Nigeria; the next tier was experienced seamen from the other West African colonies, but mainly from Sierra Leone. The third tier was Africans employed from Liverpool. The highest, best-paid tier, the only one to which the Maritime Board rates applied, was White seamen. During World War II when the government had taken over all shipping and virtually controlled pay-scales as well, this discriminatory system was retained. Even the War Risk Bonus was higher for Whites than for Blacks on Elder Dempster ships.

It should be noted that the system was accepted even by the International Labour Organisation, which noted without any criticism, that "certain shipping companies prefer to employ Chinese, Lascar and West African crews for a variety of reasons (ie, lower wages) which have obtained for many years, but apart from these long established practices, the foreign and coloured seamen are treated the same as British ...seamen."[16]

In 1940 some of the African crew of two Elder Dempster ships, the Accra and the Abosso went on strike in Liverpool, demanding higher (but not equal) wages. They also raised a perennial grievance, that Elders deducted 4/6 per week (about 22 pence; a large proportion of a weekly wage of about £1.50) from the men's wages for accommodation in the company's hostel, whether the men slept there or not![17] The men were supported by Pastor Ekarte, who, probably on the advice of the London-based Trinidadian George Padmore, circulated the men's demands to all the government and Liverpool City departments concerned with seafarers. The Pastor also contacted the National Council for Civil Liberties. Despite a flurry of activities, once all the officials realised that the Pastor had no real power and that news of the strike could be prevented from reaching West Africa, it was decided that nothing had to be done to equalise wages.

Elder Dempster attempted to take revenge by demanding from the compliant Ministry of Shipping that it get MI5, the secret intelligence service, to investigate Pastor Daniels. Though for a while there were hopes of deportation, in the end the Pastor was left alone, and in Britain.[18] Obviously, if nothing had been found to incriminate the Pastor, something could have been manufactured, so the question is, why was this not done? Did the government, especially the Colonial Office, fear that the deportation of a religious and community leader, who was well known to African bishops and secular leaders, would be politically unwise, especially as the government's compliance in racial inequities would have been disclosed?

It is likely that what the company now did was spread rumours. There are negative tales still circulating in Liverpool about Pastor Daniels which are never backed up by any oral or other evidence.

One tale is that the Pastor ran a gambling den at the Mission. Undoubtedly, the men playing cards, dominoes or billiards bet on their games as they had done on board ship. This is not sufficient to constitute a 'gambling den'.

The second tale is that Pastor Daniels procured prostitutes. This is the most amazing allegation as in any port prostitutes are easily available – all a man needs is the money to pay. There can be few seamen who cannot get directions from their shipmates to the street corners, cafes or brothels that exist in every port in the world. Mr Laryea, who frequently called in to Liverpool in the 1930s on the Elder Dempster ships on which he worked as a steward, ridicules these allegations. "There was certainly no gambling at the Mission, not while I was there... We all knew on which corners you could pick up whores." But most West Africans, Mr Laryea maintains, were interested in meeting "respectable" girls at dances at the Grafton Rooms and those organised by "Joker. (Joker Williams is well remembered as one of the earliest Black entrepreneurs; later he owned the Edge Lane Club, now the Devonshire House Hotel.)

The third charge is that the Pastor used the Mission to enrich himself. Pastor Daniels died in a council flat without having made a will; as no-one filed a probate to claim any possessions, he must have died without owning anything of value.

It is quite possible that Elder Dempster, having been unsuccessful in attempting to have him deported, spread rumours about the Pastor in the hopes of discrediting him in the eyes of the Black community and those who supported the Mission. Ivor Cummings, a Colonial Office Welfare Officer, believed that Pastor Daniels was "not very popular in shipping company circles on account of the attitude he has adopted regarding the policy of Elder Dempster... He has also incurred the displeasure of the police although they make no specific charges against him". The League of Coloured People agreed with this assessment: "Vested interests at first tried to buy him out, and then close him down... But he has triumphed against all the powers that be."[19]

In early 1945 in an interview in *Wasu Magazine* (March), Dr Udo Udoma reported that the Pastor had not given up the struggle for seamen's rights, but he did not explain what the Pastor was doing. "West African seamen have to stay under police supervision while in port, and cannot change employers. That, you'll appreciate", the Pastor told Dr Udoma, "is a very curious practice and savours of an attempt to restrict the liberty of individuals. I've always maintained that as long as Englishmen are living in Africa, so long are Africans entitled to come to, and if necessary live in any part of Britain... I understand that the Nigerian government is taking up the matter."

We know little of Pastor Daniels' contacts with West African governments, clerics or political leaders. As some clerics and members of the National Council of Nigeria and the Cameroons had visited the Mission, we know that the Mission was known to West African political figures. As mentioned previously, Dr Nnamdi Azikiwe, one of the leaders of the NCNC, knew the Pastor. Did he support the burgeoning nationalist, Pan-African and independence movements? According to Philip Osisiogu, who knew Pastor Daniels from the late 1940s, he "supported the nationalist movement, but always mixed it with Christianity".

NOTES AND REFERENCES

This chapter is partly based on letters I received in response to a request for information in the *Liverpool Echo*, and on subsequent interviews with my correspondents and other informants recommended to me. Without them this enterprise would have failed and we would not have been able to restore Daniels Ekarte to his rightful place in the history of Black peoples in Liverpool. I am most grateful to and want again to express my heartfelt thanks to them all. The correspondence and interviews took place between May 1992 and December 1993. The list of interviewees is given in the front of this book.

1. **I am grateful to Mr G.A. Coombe, and his assistant, of The Scout Association, for sending me information regarding the formation and the closure of the Troop**. Mrs Adam is listed in an undated (c. 1946/47) report of the African Churches Mission.
2. Interviews with Mrs Coca Clarke, Manchester, 1/2/1993 and Mrs Addy Ankrah, Liverpool, 23/8/1992.
3. The vast majority of the Colonial Office's files dealing with the Mission have been destroyed. This information is in Register of Correspondence,

PRO: C0977/1, file 11004B/4. There is a photograph of Major Taafel of the US Army at the Mission in the *Liverpool Daily Post* 22/12/1943. The caption states: "Major Taafel presenting toys at a *picaninnies* party...". (emphasis mine)

4. Pastor Ekarte's Ledger is in the possession of Mr Edmund Ankrah, who not only allowed me to see the original but photocopied it all for me. **There are no words to express my thanks to all the members of the Ankrah family, who have extended friendship to a total stranger – as well as sharing their memories and memorabilia of the Mission with me.** From an entry in the Ledger it would appear that there were different ledgers for different funds, but these other ledgers are apparently lost.

5. Ethel Fegan, West African Girls in England', n.d. (c.1937), manuscript in the Ethel Fegan Papers, Girton College, Cambridge.

6. *West Africa*, 3/2/1934 and 10/2/1934. I have not been able to discover whether there was any truth in the City Council's allegation of an increase in the number of stowaways, which was based on a supposed increase in the numbers of 'coloured' men signing on for Public Assistance (the dole/ unemployment benefit). If there had been an increase, it was probably due to the slump in shipping. Moreover, as young stowaway Charles Hanson was supported for six months by the Mission when he was released from prison, it would seem that stowaways were not eligible for the dole. In September 1934 there were only 36 Africans receiving the dole in Liverpool, according to the report of the British Social Hygiene Council in PRO: HO213/ 308.

7. Interview with Dr Nwafor Orizu, 8/3/1994, Nnewi, Nigeria, Dr Orizu eventually became the president of the Nigerian Senate. Dr Azikiwe, who had passed through Britain on his way to and from the USA where he had studied at a number of universities, was in 1939 the owner/editor of the *West African Pilot*; he became independent Nigeria's first President

8. It appears that Mrs Roberts had been living with a Mr Morris, another Nigerian. Mr Morris suggested to her that she should help out at the Mission. She did, and eventually moved into the Mission. Mr Morris went to remonstrate with Pastor Daniels, who would not listen. Mr Morris then enlisted the aid of other Nigerians, and the Calabar men went to try to persuade the Pastor of the error of his ways. He would not listen to them either. This led to a rift between Pastor Daniels and some of the Black community. Those who took their religious beliefs seriously objected to a pastor "taking another man's wife". Black women, though admitting that Mrs Roberts worked hard, did not like her. Some suspected that she may have thought she would have a financially more secure life at the Mission than with Mr Morris.

9. The ambivalence of some Liverpool Whites towards the city's Black citizens is exemplified by the *Daily Post*. It was usually the *Post* which carried news of Black peoples, yet, as previously mentioned, much of what it printed was racist. Another example of this is to be found in 1937, when the paper's foreign news pages were often devoted to Hitler's eugenicist atrocities in Europe. The question of 'race' was frequently discussed in this context,

and 'race-hatred' was written of as abhorrent. Yet a book review was entitled "Nigger's View of Liverpool"! (Post, 21/10/1937)

10. For two years, 1934 and 1935 news of the Mission appeared on a number of occasions in *West Africa*, but from 1936 the Mission vanished from this weekly journal's pages. This is interesting as it was in 1936 that the firm of West African Newspapers merged with the Nigerian Printing and Publishing Co., the owners/publishers of the influential *Nigerian Daily Times*. One of the owners of the NPP Co. was Elder Dempster, the Liverpool-based shipping company, which published a weekly called *West African Review*. It is probable that by 1936 Elder Dempster also owned *West Africa* as by then Mr R.B. Paul was chairperson of West African Newspapers and in charge of both the British-based weeklies as well as the Lagos newspaper.

R.B. Paul was, for some time in the 1930s, the treasurer of the Mission, but we do not know exactly when. Thus, in the late 1930s, when he was in charge of this stable of newspapers, he must have known Pastor Daniels. Why then did *West Africa* not carry news of the Mission? Was Paul carrying out Elder Dempster's instructions? Curiously, Paul left the papers (ie, Elder Dempster) in about 1940 and accepted an appointment as Port Welfare Officer for the Ministry of Labour, Why leave such a highly paid powerful post for that of a lowly civil servant?

11. W.J. O'Donovan MP forwarded Frank Crosby's letter to the Home Office, who then requested information from the chief constables. Liverpool's Assistant Chief Constable Winstanley replied on 17/4/1934 that "there had been cases in the past... Too easy for coloured men to become domiciled... But there are no 'rings of white slave traffickers."

The replies from the other chief constables also differentiated between brothel-keeping, procuring young girls, and sexual relations between Black men and White women, which they all deplored. The Home Office decided that no action was required. The internal memoranda in the files are very revealing. For example, before the reports arrived, one official with an illegible signature wrote that while brothel keeping could be dealt with by the magistrates, "the association of coloured men with white women is already causing serious social consequences in Liverpool, Cardiff, South Shields and elsewhere". His colleagues were obviously expected to understand what he was talking about, without it having to be stated. After the chief constables' reports arrived, another official noted that "all we can do is to discourage coloured seamen from obtaining British passports *so that we can treat them as aliens when they get here to prevent them remaining, and the position becoming worse*". (emphasis mine)

Frank Crosby to Dr W.J. O'Donovan, n.d., and internal memorandum over illegible signature, 26/3/1934, PRO: H045/ 25404/175483/10. Replies from chief constables, April 1934 and internal memorandum by ?, B.H., 3/7/1934, PRO: H045/25404/174583/11.

12. See also *The Keys*, 2/1, 1934, pp. 1, 20; 2/2, 1934, p.31. On the League of Coloured People, see Peter Fryer, *Staying Power*, Pluto Press, 1984, pp.326-334. The Negro Welfare Association is thus far undocumented, as are the activities of Harry O'Connell, though I make some reference to him in my

'Racism and Resistance: Cardiff in the 1930s and 1940s', *Llafur*, 5/4, 1991, esp. pp.60-61. The *Negro Worker*, published by the International Trade Union Committee of Negro Workers in Hamburg, was an 'arm' of the Profintern, a section of the Communist International. Otto Huiswoud succeeded George Padmore as editor of the *Worker* in 1934, after George Padmore's resignation. On Padmore see James Hooker, *Black Revolutionary*, London, 1967.

13. *Liverpool Daily Post*, 6/8/1934.
    It is not possible to determine why there is a gap of ten months between the resolution and the arrival of the petition at the Colonial Office. As the CO's file has been destroyed, the contents of the petition are also unknown. That it was sent to the CO is evident from Correspondence Register PRO: C0713/11, file 46011/11. Reports of the special service are in West Africa 10/8/1935 and *Liverpool Daily Post*, 7/8/1935.

14. Flyer in George Padmore's fifth book of press cuttings, Padmore Research Library, Accra. (It is possible that I made a mistake copying the date as there is an advertisement for this service in the *Liverpool Daily Post*, 10/10/1937.)

15. In West Africa Elder Dempster owned coaling, lighterage, wharf and engineering companies. For many years it had the monopoly for carrying mail and bullion to the West African colonies. It was also the parent company of the Bank of British West Africa, now Standard Chartered. For information on the strike and its consequences and for more on the power of this company in West Africa and Liverpool, see my forthcoming 'Strike! Elder Dempster and West African Seamen 1940-1941', *Immigrants & Minorities*, (forthcoming, July 1994). A fuller version of this paper was presented at the conference on 'Ethnic Seafarers', Liverpool University, December 1992.

16. International Labour Office, 'Seamen's Welfare in Ports', 1939, PRO: C0859/11/7.

17. As n.15.

18. Mr Guttery (Ministry of Shipping) to J.J. Paskin (Colonial Office) 1/10/1940, PRO: C0859/40/2.

19. Report by Ivor Cummings 6/10/1941, PRO: C0859/76/10; League of Coloured People's *Newsletter*, August 1942, pp. 102-3.

Pastor Ekarte in 1946

Some of the children outside the Mission in 1946. Note how the Mission buildings had deteriorated during the war.

Pastor Ekarte with members of a lodge(?). Nobody has been able to identify the lodge. Reginald Ankrah is on the far right. *(By courtesy of Reeves/NMGM)*

Pastor Ekarte and some of the Black community at the reception for Paul Robeson in St. George's Hall, 1948. Pastor Ekarte is upper left. *(By courtesy of Reeves/NMGM)*

CHAPTER FIVE

The Mission becomes a children's home, 1944-1949

Illegitimate children born during the war

In its 28 July 1945 issue the liberal (and clearly racist) weekly *New Statesman and Nation* carried an article headed "War Babies". It described the young mothers in a village, "9 out of 10 unmarried", who had children by soldiers stationed in the area during the war. It was "rare for the fathers to support them". One girl in a neighbouring village "pushes a pram that contains the most engaging picaninny ever seen, a sparkling black bastard".

A few months later a leading African-American newspaper raised the same issue from a somewhat different perspective. The US army discouraged intermarriage between Black soldiers and White women, W.E.B. DuBois had written, which resulted in the birth of illegitimate children. Dr DuBois, a Black sociologist, estimated that the total number in the UK would be between one and two thousand. (Dr DuBois had just returned from Britain where he had attended the Pan-African Congress in Manchester.) A year later a Baltimore weekly Black newspaper quoted another estimate of 2000 "brown babies", probably with similar numbers in Italy and others in France and Germany. The paper told a story of a White British husband who, on finding on his return from the war that his wife had had a 'coloured' baby, painted the child white.[1]

[There is some lack of clarity about the US military's position/ regarding inter-racial marriage. Trinidad-born Learie Constantine, the famous cricketer, claimed that the "US military authorities absolutely forbade marriage under any circumstances between their coloured troops and white women in England".[2] As he was a Ministry of Labour welfare officer working in the Liverpool district during the war, Constantine was in a position to know what was actually happening. Historian Graham Smith could not discover written instructions forbidding intermarriage. However, he found that "the implementation of marriage regulations was left to local American officers, certain of whom held strong views on the association of blacks and whites".[3] There were 130,000 African-Americans among the one and a half million American service-men and women who passed through or were stationed in Britain during World War II.]

Pastor Daniels gets involved

Another African-American sociologist, Dr St. Clair Drake, then carrying out research among Cardiff's Black population, visited the Mission in 1947, apparently at the instigation of the Anti-Slavery Society. He reported that the Pastor had become concerned about the illegitimate babies resulting from the presence of many thousands of allied troops in the UK. As early as 1942 Pastor Daniels had approached both the US army authorities and the British government, proposing that a special fund should be set up for the care of such children. He was ignored. During the war, Pastor Daniels told St. Clair Drake, he "attempted to do what he could in helping women with coloured illegitimate babies to make an adjustment".[4]

That no attention had been paid to the Pastor's warning is made clear in a letter written on 5 October 1945 to Quaker philanthropist Miss M. Fry by a Mrs Russell, of Stockton, Warwickshire. It seems that Mrs Russell intended to provide a home for the children whose mothers wanted to give them up. She explained that the Pastor had "a house full of these poor unwanted children given into his charge by their unfortunate mothers – sometimes they were left on his doorstep. His small house is much overcrowded with a very long waiting list, and for this reason the Local Authorities cannot help him, on the grounds that it would only encourage him to keep these little mites, some coloured, some white, in a congested and squalid locality. So poor Pastor Ekarte is carrying on his difficult work without Public Assistance." How Mrs Russell came to know Pastor Daniels or why she was so concerned with the fate of these children is not known.[5]

The Booker T. Washington Children's Home

In June 1945 Pastor Daniels circulated a printed appeal seeking funds for a 'Booker-T-Washington Children's Home', "to accommodate 40 to 50 children of coloured American soldiers, Africans, and West Indian soldiers and technicians". He explained that recent reports showed that 7% of all births were illegitimate.[6] The mothers were mainly teenagers, but "the great problem was married English women whose husbands are serving abroad". It was particularly these married women he wanted to help: in most cases, especially when the illegitimate child was 'coloured', the returned husband would only "take back" his wife if the child was got rid of.

He had formed a committee to raise funds for the proposed home. George Padmore was chairman and Learie Constantine was the secretary.[7] It would appear that enough money was raised in 1945 to enable the Committee to search for a suitable building. When one was found at Roundhay in Leeds, Pastor Daniels was so excited that he immediately asked Ivor Cummings and J.L. Keith (The Colonial Office's Welfare Officers) to be on the home's governing board.[8] However, when the contract was about to be signed, it was discovered that the building could not be used for the purpose intended. The purchase had to be abandoned. The search was renewed, but without success. According to Constantine, all was not as it seemed: "There was opposition when we looked elsewhere... I was unhappy at this further experience of furtive opposition to any effort to help these coloured children, condemned to illegitimacy by a distant Government".

The Booker T. Washington Children's Home committee wound up its affairs. "The money raised was, by common consent, devoted to other charitable purposes, partly for coloured people and including the Royal Infirmary at Liverpool. We had a bank manager as treasurer and everything was wound up in legal order", Learie Constantine wrote sadly and angrily in his *Colour Bar*.[9]

But the Pastor did not give up. Another committee was set up in 1948 and Padmore it seems, was again a member. Without asking her consent, the Pastor also appointed Dr Kitty Fraser, then a general medical practitioner who also worked for the Child

Welfare and Maternity Clinics. Dr Fraser was well aware of the "children resulting from liaisons between American soldiers and white girls from the district, for whom neither government wanted responsibility". However, as meetings were held without all the committee being informed and as she thought the "scheme was doubtful and hare-brained and that the Pastor had become a tool in the hands of unscrupulous people", she withdrew. Other Liverpool people on the committee at this time were Mrs A. Carruthers and Mrs S. Tyler; Messrs E.O. Eyo, J.U. Davis, V. James and A. Vanderpuije.[10]

The children remain at the Mission

In 1946 the US journal *Liberty* (7/12/1946) found six "waifs" at the Mission in Hill Street, aged from 15 months to three years, looked after by "two overworked matron-housekeepers". The reporter described the Mission as a "small, poor building", which was not allowed by the health authorities to take more children. Pastor Ekarte's dream was of a home "to accommodate the estimated 600 children of coloured fathers in Great Britain". In the meanwhile, he was paying for the maintenance of some children "farmed out in nearby towns", He hoped "to come to America to appeal for funds".

In August 1947 St. Clair Drake found eight children at the Mission, who "seemed healthy and well fed, but the rather old building had neither the sanitary conveniences nor the trained personnel to carry out 'a social work job', according to the best standards of either American or English social agencies. Father Ekarte stated that he had over a hundred children on his waiting list and that they had been 'placed around in various homes'."

Drake's report was seen by the Anti-Slavery Society and its president, C.W.W. Greenidge, wrote to the Pastor. Though this letter has not been preserved, Pastor Daniels in his response clarified the number of children concerned: 8 lived at the Mission; 25 were supported in foster homes; there were 158 on his waiting list.[12]

News of the children even reached Australia. The *Women's Weekly* described them as "sturdy and happy". Pastor Daniels told the Weekly that he wanted the children to "grow up with the same pride and the same opportunities as other children have". In the US, the weekly magazine *Ebony* devoted three pages to photographs of the Mission and the story of "fatherless children". There was discrimination by adoption societies, which had been drawn to the attention of the British government, but nothing had been done to rectify the situation, according to *Ebony*. The US army had "denied permission to marry to hundreds of Negro GIs who wanted to accept the obligations of fatherhood... Reverend Ekarte was the children's adopted father in every way except legally. He is loved by the children in the Liverpool nursery... White women are matrons who look after the children... The African Churches Mission has been struggling along on very limited finances."[13]

The matrons mentioned in these articles were the Mission's housekeeper, Mrs Roberts and her mother, who had also moved to the Mission during the war. Mrs Roberts' two eldest daughters also joined her for a while, and they also helped. The neighbours also gave a hand. Mrs O'Brien remembers that her "daughter was then about ten years old, after school would bring a pram to our front door with two beautiful babies in it to mind them for a time and then take them back to the mission." The already overworked younger Roberts girls, Rita and Rose, now had additional washing and cleaning to do before and after work: "me and my sister had to do all the babies' washing – loads of nappies every day and bedding for all the cots".

Fundraising in the US

This is the most problematic episode in the story of the "brown babies", as they were often called. On 4 April 1947 the London *Daily Mail* printed an interview with a Mr E.B. Kendall, solicitor of the Negro Welfare Association of London and Liverpool, regarding what it called "dusky problem babies". Mr Kendall is reported as saying that the Association, of which Edwin DuPlan was secretary, was planning to charter a liner to take 5,000 'coloured' babies to the US, "to save them growing up as social misfits". Mrs Roosevelt, "was interested in the scheme and was organising funds in the US". Mr Kendall apparently concluded by saying that "we're making arrangements in this country for the other 5,000 coloured babies who'll be left".

There are some very strange aspects to this newspaper story. First of all, presumably the association mentioned by the reporter was in fact the Negro Welfare Centre, which was not in London but in Manchester. Secondly, would a solicitor make an unsubstantiated public statement, especially one involving a world-famous figure such as Mrs Eleanor Roosevelt? (Everyone had presumed that the Mrs Roosevelt mentioned was the wife of the recently deceased US president.) Thirdly, why didn't any other British newspaper pick up this story?[14]

The US Embassy in London was immediately asked by the US State Department to investigate these claims. The Department had "doubts about the practicality and social desirability of the plan... The numbers of children quoted greatly exceeds previous information." The Embassy made enquiries and discovered that Mr Kendall had been seeking an interview with the Home Office to discuss the issue. The Embassy also discussed the article with the League of Coloured People's acting president, Dr M. Joseph-Mitchell, who advised that the maximum number of such children was 650. He believed Mr Kendall to have been the "dupe or accomplice of DuPlan and paster Ekarte". The Mission in Liverpool was caring for eight children, but this was "reportedly window-dressing for a swindle".[15]

Scotland Yard, asked for information by the Embassy, advised that "Ekarte had previously come to the unfavourable notice of the police". The firm of Kendall & Rigby was reputable, but Eddie DuPlan was not. DuPlan, a half-caste", was running disreputable clubs in Liverpool, Manchester and Cardiff, which were financed by a West African, James Eggay Taylor. The men, the police claimed, had set up the Negro Welfare Centre "ostensibly to look after coloured people but which was nothing better than a profit-making lodging house at which coloured men were charged high prices and received very little in return... The welfare was DuPlan and Taylor's own." Ekarte held no position in the Centre; his record in "Negro welfare in Liverpool is an unsavoury one... (He is) interested in his own personal gain", the police report concluded.[16]

Contrary to these police allegations against Pastor Daniels, the Foreign Office informed the Embassy that it had no "adverse information" on either the Pastor or the Mission. Mr Ekarte had written to them in January to advise that he intended sending DuPlan to the US to solicit for funds for a children's home.

The Embassy now asked the US Consul in Liverpool to interview Mr Kendall and Daniels Ekarte. At the interview on May 12th Pastor Daniels confirmed that he had sent DuPlan to the US to raise funds to support the 150 or so children of Black US servicemen in the Liverpool area. He had eight living at the Mission and would use surplus funds to establish a larger home. He estimated that there were probably 5,000 illegitimate babies altogether – Black and White. He did not know how or why the *Daily Mail* had so exaggerated the numbers of 'coloured children, of whom he thought there were about 500.[17]

Had the Pastor ever been party to the *Mail*'s exaggerations? There are no inaccurate statements attributed to him personally. For example, the estimate of 600 'coloured' illegitimate children that he gave *Liberty* magazine is quite close to the estimate he gave the US Consul. Neither does the Pastor appear to have envisaged wholesale transportation. "It is impossible without some agreement between the British and US governments... An enquiry bureau to sift applications is necessary. You can't just post a child off to America like a parcel", he told the *Australian Women's Weekly.*

While the diplomats were gathering information and misinformation on Pastor Daniels, Eddie DuPlan was in the US. On 25 January 1947 the *New York Amsterdam News* reported on a press conference at which DuPlan (or the newspaper) again exaggerated the numbers of children. Eighty were said to be at the Mission, 40 in other homes in Liverpool and another 1,600 scattered around the UK. Neither the UK nor the US government had made any plans for dealing with these children. DuPlan was in the US to raise $100,000 (£25,000) for a home. The New York Urban League (a Black civic organisation) would be helping to set up a committee of "Negro and White citizens" to aid the effort.[18] DuPlan also attempted to enlist the aid of another equally respected Black organisation, the National Association for the Advancement of Colored People (NAACP).

The first alarms about exaggerations were probably raised by the League of Coloured People's president, Dr Harold Moody. Dr Moody, returning from a visit home to Jamaica, stopped in the US to attempt to raise funds for a League cultural project. Dr Joseph-Mitchell, at his meeting with the US Embassy officials in London in mid-April told Embassy staff that "the League was greatly concerned and Dr Moody was doing everything possible in the US to discredit DuPlan". At a meeting in Harlem in early April Dr Moody reduced the media's "thousands" of children to about 500, 150 of whom, he claimed, were being cared for in children's homes.[19]

It might have been Dr Moody's counter-propaganda that led the NAACP's secretary to ask George Padmore for information. (Walter White had met Padmore on his visit to the UK in 1944.) Padmore replied in a confidential letter that Taylor and DuPlan had indeed run "dubious night clubs" in Manchester and Liverpool. After the war business "had evaporated", and as he was in trouble with the police, Taylor had returned to the Gold Coast. DuPlan was "left holding the baby and, seeking a way to cover himself, made approaches to Pastor Ekarte and arranged to represent him in America." Padmore described Ekarte as a "Christian honestly concerned with the welfare of these children". DuPlan had sought a mandate from the Pan-African Federation, but this had been refused. However, the cause of illegitimate children was urgent, and Padmore urged the NAACP to support the efforts of the League of Coloured People. Padmore also sent White a copy of a story on the children which he had just sent to the *Chicago Defender*.[20]

The escalating numbers and publicity led some Black and White Americans to reject the proposal to import large numbers of illegitimate children of mixed-parentage.[21] There was at least one most unfortunate repercussion to DuPlan's (or the media's) exaggerations. Joe Louis, the world heavy-weight champion boxer, had decided to donate $1,000 to the Mission for the children's home. His wife went to visit and found "nothing like I'd been led to believe". She had expected to find 185 orphans in an orderly, clean home, and instead found five "ragged and undernourished tots in an unkempt place with none of the facilities you'd expect to find in a nursery", Undoubtedly, to the eyes of a wealthy American woman, unfamiliar with conditions in post-war Britain, that is how the Mission looked. Mrs Louis had been led to believe by the US media that there were 20,000 "Tan-Yank war babies". On her advice Joe Louis held the $1,000 "in reserve to allow Father Ekarte, if he so desires, to forward an explanation of the conditions" his wife had found at the Mission.[22]

Early in May the British Information Service in the US issued a statement denying that there were any plans to ship children to the US and confirmed that the numbers were about 500. The State Department, which admitted it had a report on the matter, refused to release it, on the grounds that it was not involved in the issue. A Miss M. Scheider of the New York State Welfare Department wrote to the British Family Welfare Association in 1947 to enquire if the Mission had permission to fundraise in the USA. The National Urban League disassociated itself, and the New York Urban League denied that it had ever endorsed the venture. However, the New York Urban League Executive Director told the *Amsterdam News* that whatever the true numbers of children and the veracity of DuPlan, "the important point is what is to happen to the children... The British and American governments have a clear responsibility to work on this problem together"[23]

Bureaucrats consider adoption

In order to try to determine the actual numbers of children involved, the League of Coloured People had commissioned a survey. (The League must have decided on this course of action after the Save the Children Fund had refused to undertake a survey because the Ministry of Health would not subsidise it.) In what the League admitted was an undercount, the survey discovered 544 illegitimate children of mixed-parentage. British bureaucracy regarding adoption was frustrating those fathers, and African-

American families, who had volunteered to adopt children, the survey noted.[24]

At a meeting at the Home Office early in 1946 where the League's report was discussed, the Home Secretary worried about the "appalling discrimination" in the US – would the children be happier there, he wondered. There was less discrimination in England. In his own constituency of South Shields there were 144 such children, and parents and teachers had just rejected a proposal to put them in a segregated school. In any case the children were British subjects and would need US permission to land and could only be adopted by a British subject or a relative who was not the putative father. Another official worried whether Britain should "countenance the assumption that there is no place for people of colour in the UK". The political implications of "establishing a coloured British minority in the US would have to be considered.[25]

This self-righteous prevarication led to masterly inaction. In January 1947 Reginald Sorensen MP, often the parliamentary mouthpiece of the Pan-African Federation and other anti-imperialist organisations, asked in Parliament what the government was doing regarding the children. The Labour Government's Christopher Mayhew, Under Secretary of State at the Foreign Office, replied that he was "studying the question". A year later Lt Thomas C. Skeffington-Lodge, the Labour MP for Bedford, asked in the House whether arrangements had been made and welfare safeguards put in place for the adoption of illegitimate (including 'coloured') children by US families. The Home Secretary, James Ede, replied that the question had been "under consideration for some time". (It had indeed – for two years!) If full enquiries on both sides of the Atlantic showed that adoption by the American relatives would be in the child's favour, he saw no objections.[26] (It is difficult to understand British bureaucracy's insistence that American adoptive parents had to be relatives. After all, in the UK the children either languished in orphanages, or at times were sent to inappropriate foster homes (see below).

By mid-1948, with added pressure from the American Branch of the International Social Service, British bureaucrats relented a little. According to the *Los Angeles Criterion* of 24 August 1948, blood relatives and families "which could prove to the Local Welfare Board that they could care for the child in a 'good moral atmosphere, and which accepted supervision by the Board", would be allowed to apply to adopt children of mixed-parentage. The children would be counted as part of the USA's British immigration quota.

The children at the Mission

While officials were contemplating British self-esteem and political considerations, Pastor Daniels' hopes for US cash to help him open his dream home had been dashed. As the Pastor wrote to St. Clair Drake on 28 October 1947, "DuPlan has now returned as empty handed as he went over". He now had 158 children on the Mission's list and begged Drake to help him raise $12,000 for buildings he had just seen which could accommodate 500 children.[27]

Meanwhile the Pastor had informed the Colonial Office Welfare Department that he was caring for some children. On 5 April 1946, Pastor Daniels also wrote to the Ministry of Health, asking why no-one had visited the Mission as Mr J.L. Keith of the Colonial Office, Mrs Russell and Miss Alma LaBadie, a Jamaican journalist then attached to the Royal Air Force, had spoken with the Ministry on behalf of the Mission. It seems that the Colonial Office's Welfare Department had been co-operating in some fashion with the Ministry of Health, whom the League of Coloured People had also contacted in 1945.[28]

In March 1944, after a foster mother had complained that a child had been removed from her and placed with the Mission, a Liverpool Health Visitor called at Hill Street. She advised Pastor Daniels on how to make the formal notification of the reception of children. This permitted the Pastor to apply for a grant from the local authority. His application was rejected on the grounds of overcrowding. The Pastor refused to reduce the number of children to the four demanded by the authority. Despite this lack of financial support, the Health Visitor and Dr Ruby Bell, who visited regularly, found the children well fed and cared for.

Mrs Reeves and Mrs Phillips, who as young girls had done so much of the housework at the Mission, remember that the Pastor also took in neglected children. One child had been taken away from a foster mother who had just left him in a cot all day. He had come to the Mission "almost deformed, with his legs and arms all curled". He was given a therapeutic bath every day but it took a year for him to be able to walk. Could it have been this foster mother who had complained?

It is difficult to understand the Pastor's complaint that no-one from the Ministry of Health had visited the Mission, as in February 1946 a Ms R.W. Whiteway, a "Woman Inspector" for the North West Region of the Ministry had called. She reported that the "most appropriate description of this place is that it represents the general appearance of a mother and her eight children in a private household in reduced financial circumstances". Mrs Roberts was being helped by relatives. Pastor Ekarte, whom she thought an extremely amiable man... appears to be well known everywhere... The local hospitals and institutions communicate with him regarding the placing of these children". The Pastor had showed her a list of nearly one hundred mothers who were waiting to place their "illegitimate coloured children" and he was maintaining 18 children, of whom eight were living at the Mission.[29]

In her report Ms Whiteway also stated that she had met Dr Bell, Senior Medical Officer in charge of Child Welfare and Dr Williams, the Senior Assistant Medical Officer in Birkenhead. These officials told her that the known illegitimate "coloured' children were being cared for by their mothers. There had been 175 born in Liverpool in 1944-45. "It might be possible", Dr Bell added, "to offer a few places at the residential nurseries if the need arises." This hopeful assessment was of course contradicted by what Ms Whiteway had learned from her visit to the Mission. It was also contradicted in an interview the Ministry had conducted the previous year with Miss Devling, the welfare worker at the Stanley House nursery. (See chapter 9) She had said that "her main problem was the placing of coloured children, particularly those who are illegitimate, whose mothers cannot look after them.

It is almost impossible to find foster parents, and both the voluntary organisations and the local public assistance authority find it difficult, owing to the shortage of accommodation, to admit children to their homes".[30] It would appear therefore that the local authority officials were ignorant of the real situation. Or they simply were not interested?

In May Ms Whiteway again visited the Mission, possibly because a baby had died of gastro-enteritis, despite all medical efforts. At this interview Pastor Daniels described his aims in detail. "It is his intention to set up a Home for about 100 coloured children, these children to attend the local elementary schools, and at the eligible age enter for the scholarship examination. Those children who do not pass will then be transferred to a residential school where they will be given technical training... Such residential schools or colleges to be set up later as the scheme develops... In effect he would like to establish a coloured population such as exists in America... A scheme which envisages the setting up of training schools, colleges and Universities for coloured people." The Pastor, Ms Whiteway concluded, "talked very bitterly about the treatment of the coloured adolescent and adult population in Liverpool. He stated that the majority of them are now out of work, and that even when they are in work, the wages are so low that a married man is unable to support a family... Pastor Ekarte looked rather depressed and despondent when I met him, but I think the death of the baby weighed considerably on his mind."[31]

Officials continued to visit. Dr Wright of the Home Office visited in May 1947, but no copies of his report have survived. He and Dr Makepeace were there again a year later, in May 1948. They found the children clean and adequately dressed and "bright and alert". They also found some safety problems and criticised the state of the bedrooms and the kitchen, and a "general lack of management". On their return to London, Dr Wright noted that "the environment had deteriorated" since his previous visit.[32]

During May the Liverpool Society for the Prevention of Cruelty to Children (LSPCC), having received a letter of complaint, also visited the Mission. In the report the Society sent to the Home

Office, the LSPCC inspector described the children as "clean and fairly well nourished", but the kitchen, yard and bedding were dirty. "I have visited a good many low down lodging houses", the Inspector wrote, "but have never found one as dirty as this". The LSPCC questioned the efficiency of the Home Office: "we are informed you do inspect, and have approved the Mission as a temporary home".[33]

Meanwhile Dr Ruby Bell tried to exert some indirect pressure on the Colonial Office to assume some responsibility. She wrote that the children were not undernourished or ragged, but the Mission was dirty; it was a pity it was not run by "a good committee at a higher standard". A now probably desperate Daniels Ekarte wrote twice to the Colonial Office asking for a recommendation to be sent to Professor Drake, now back in the US, to support his plea for funds.[34]

This pressure resulted in Dr Wright inspecting the Mission again on June 7th. He found the children "clean and obviously happy... No evidence of neglect...but squalid environment and lamentably poor standard of home management... Primitive washing arrangements, overcrowded bedroom (Mrs Roberts and seven children all slept in one small room)... No outdoor play area". Dr Wright noted, as he had previously, that the cafe is the primary source of income" for the Mission. (On the cafe, the Cocoa Rooms, see chapter 8.)

[It was probably this – having to run the cafe in order to have an income – that resulted in "poor home management". Mrs Roberts and her mother, with the help of her two daughters in the evenings, had to cook, serve and clean in the Mission and in the Cocoa Rooms and to look after the toddlers. Though sometimes there were other Roberts relatives around to help, there were still not enough pairs of hands to keep the increasingly dilapidated Mission building as spic and span as it had been in the pre-war years.]

Dr Wright repeated his previous suggestion that the Pastor should attempt to secure financial aid from voluntary bodies or the Army authorities. This was a somewhat futile suggestion as Pastor Daniels must already have done that. So had the League of Coloured People, but even this well-connected organisation failed to raise enough money to keep open the Rainbow Home, which it had helped establish. The real question is, why didn't the Home Office help? Children were, after all, its responsibility.

Subsequent to this visit Dr Wright wrote officially to Mr Ekarte asking if he had definite plans for moving the children to another home as the Hill Street building was "environmentally unsuitable".[35]

The Home Office inspectors appear to have been divided in their opinion about the Mission. Dr Makepeace, who had visited in 1947, thought it was a case of "just a group of children living happily in slum conditions", Mr MacGregor advised that as Mr Ekarte received donations, the Mission had to be classified as a "voluntary home and was thus subject to Home Office inspection; the physical conditions described by Dr Makepeace could not be tolerated even if the children were alright. This led to a Mr Revell ordering a "full inspection with recommendations"; he also wanted the sources of the Mission's income ascertained.[36]

The Home Office closes the Mission Home

Home Office inspectors Ms Woodall and Mr Woodlock arrived at the Mission on 22 February 1949. They found broken windows, broken linoleum, not enough chairs for the children to sit to eat – in fact such unsuitable conditions that they promptly withdrew the registration the Pastor had obtained the previous November. The two inspectors commented that the Pastor was "coloured and his English is not standard in either accent or construction... His concern is sincere. Could he be moved to a suitable house?" they queried their superiors.[37] (The inspectors did not explain the relevance of the colour of Pastor Daniels' skin or his "non-standard English" to the welfare of the children.)

Ignoring this suggestion from its own inspectors, in April the Home Office demanded concrete plans from Pastor Ekarte for moving the children to a suitable building. The Home Office also warned the Liverpool Town Clerk that unless the Pastor found suitable premises the Home would be closed and the children would have to be taken by the city. This resulted in the Liverpool

Children's Department doing its own somewhat belated investigation. The Department found dirty and dingy conditions, and also expressed concern about the "sizeable donations which the Pastor was said to have received. The Department recommended to the Home Office that the Missions accounts be investigated. (The Home Office inspectors had also been interested in the accounts, which the Pastor had refused to show them. But even if he had kept accounts, there was no reason for him to show them to City or Home Office officials as he had not received any funding from them.)

Though there was no suggestion of neglect and the children were found to be "happy, lively and healthy", on 31 May 1949 the Home Office issued a 28 day notice of closure. Appeals could be lodged within 14 days. On June 1st Pastor Daniels replied, pointing out that neither he nor the children's mothers had ever received a penny from the government or charitable societies. "Many homes around here are in similar condition", he wrote. Paul Robeson, the world famous singer, who had visited the home, had written promising help.

But this was to no avail. On June 3, eleven days *before* the period to lodge an appeal had expired, the Home Office acted At 7.30 am local officials and the police battered on the Mission's door. Locking the distraught Pastor in his office, the children were dragged from their beds and taken off to a city children's home.

Pastor Daniels was even barred from visiting the children, though Mrs Roberts was allowed to see them. (Mrs Roberts was, of course, White.)

Pastor Daniels turned everywhere for help. On June 16 he wrote to the King and Princess Margaret. The King passed the letter to the Home Office who sent a form for registering the new premises the Pastor had written the King he had found. The Princess replied that she could not intervene. Neither could the Colonial Office. William Gallagher MP took up the case, but the Home Office's response to him was a recounting of events. The popular *Sunday Pictorial* (12/6/1949) interviewed Pastor Daniels, who, the paper wrote, "was known to Britain's coloured population as the Black Saint of Merseyside". The Pastor said that he had appealed to the Mayor. "The Home Office say the premises are not suitable for a children's home. No-one knows that better than I. But the authority have never helped me find a better place."

The Governor of Nigeria sought information from both the Colonial Office and the Home Office. The Home Office replied with a statement of the 'facts and advised that the Mission's accounts were a mess and that the local committee could not be found. (It was not strictly true that the committee could not be found. What the Home Office had learned from the Liverpool Town Clerk, who had interviewed the committee's Assistant Secretary Mr E.O. Eyo, was that the committee had not met since the previous August.) On June 24 Pastor Daniels advised the Home Office of the premises he had just found. But the Home Office would not relent. Its officials decided that the Pastor's letters of June 1 and June 3 "could not be regarded as constituting an appeal in terms of the Act". The Pastor could not have the children back.

What happened to the children?

An officer from the Liverpool Children's Department visiting the Mount Olive Home on 27 July 1949 found the children "shy and unresponsive". Some had been moved to another home, in Fazakerley. One boy had been placed in the care of a 60-year-old couple who ran an old people's home in Sussex. The couple also had an "imbecile" son of 20. But there was no suggestion, the officer reported, that the Hales had taken the child in order to help them run the home. The Pastor was not to be allowed to visit, but Mrs Roberts could continue to see the remaining children.[38]

In the final pages of the Home Office file dealing with this sorry tale is a comment from the Parliamentary Under Secretary of State for the Home Office. He suggested to his officials that Pastor Ekarte should be visited, as he "may be a person of consequence among coloured people in Liverpool. It would be a pity if he was made more bitter over this than is necessary, or were allowed to feel that he has been penalised because of his colour." So an official visited and reported that Pastor Daniels was "distressed at the loss and indignant at manhandling by the police":[39]

Surely this experience could not but make anyone distressed and indignant. Wasn't the Pastor "penalised because of his colour"? Why was he not helped to acquire other premises? Alternately, why couldn't the Mission have been renovated? Why was the buck passed constantly between government and city departments and a sometimes punitive philanthropic organisation? Why were the children taken away before the appeal period had expired? Why were they taken from their beds? Why, when they had grown up as brothers and sisters, were they immediately separated? Why was Mrs Roberts, but not Pastor Daniels, allowed to see the children? If anyone had cared about the children, who were obviously happy and contented and looked on him as their father and on Mrs Roberts as their mother, ways would have been found to resolve the problems and deficiencies. And finally, why was the government so indifferent to the fate of the many hundreds of children of mixed-parentage when it had been warned, and had in fact discussed the likelihood of their birth and probable problems, before the US troops ever set foot in Britain?[40]

One or two of the children have remained in the Liverpool area according to Rita Reeves, who smiles as she remembers those far off days. "We had this old pram that we put four of them in to take them to the clinic... We used to take them all out in their prams and all the people used to admire them. We had them all dressed the same. My mum used to make all their clothes. We also got a lot of clothes sent from America and sweets and chocolates for the babies... The Health stepped in and they were taken away. It broke his heart to lose them. Some of them were adopted. The only one we (Rita and Rose) can remember is Brian, who was adopted by a couple in Chester. When he grew up he joined the Salvation Army." Others have appeared. If the Liverpool experience was similar to that in the rest of Britain, very few of the children were adopted or fostered. Most spent their young lives in children's homes.

NOTES AND REFERENCES

1. *Chicago Defender*, 24/11/1945; *Afro-American*, 23/11/1946.
2. Learie Constantine, *Colour Bar*, London, 1954, p.100.
3. Graham Smith, *When Jim Crow Met John Bull*, London, 1987, p.205.
4. As St. Clair Drake was researching the coloured community in Cardiff and knew Padmore and other activists, it is likely that he would have heard of Pastor Daniels without the Anti-Slavery Society. His preliminary report (the final one has not been found) was written or the Julius Rosenwald Fund, a US philanthropic organisation which had been supportive of African-Americans for many years. Drake's 'A Preliminary Statement on the Study of the Adjustment of Children Born in the British Isles to White Mothers of Fathers who Were Allegedly American Negro Soldiers', c.1948, Fisk University: Julius Rosenwald Fund Papers, Box 409, folder 2.

   That Drake visited on behalf of the Anti-Slavery Society is in Daniels Ekarte to Anti-Slavery Society, 23/8/1948, Rhodes House Library: Br. Emp. Mss. S.23, Box H3/2. Welfare agencies in seven British cities had counted 222 such children. "The number is so great in Cardiff that the staff had no time to count them", St. Clair Drake reported. A Black woman in Cardiff told him "to tell the Americans that when the next war breaks out, just keep the coloured troops at home and send along the uniforms. We have the troops here."

   Preliminary Report, p.2. The final estimate by the League of Coloured People was 780.
5. Mrs Russell to Miss M. Fry, 5/10/1945, Rhodes House Library: Br. Emp. Mss. s.23.
6. In Liverpool illegitimate births as a proportion of all births had risen from 4.8% in 1938 to 8.3% in 1944. In numbers this meant a rise from 771 to 1,274. In 1944 the infant mortality rate for illegitimate children was 97 per 1,000, almost double the rate for legitimate births, 54 per 1,000. The City Council felt impelled to increase its grant to the voluntary organisations working with unmarried mothers. *Report on the Health of the City of Liverpool during 1944*, Liverpool, 1945, pp.2, 6.
7. That Constantine and Padmore were officers of the 1945 committee is in 'Booker-T-Washington Children's Home', circular, June 1945, Rhodes House Library: Br. Emp. Mss. S.23.

   Learie Constantine was well-known for his involvement in the issue of illegitimate children of mixed parentage. Besides working with Pastor Daniels he also worked with the League of Coloured People (LCP), which in 1946 was helping the Russells set up a home. Among the few remaining papers in the possession of the Constantine family is a letter dated 18/1/1945 from Learie to Miss I. Hillyer, a Health Visitor in Essex. Miss Hillyer had written to John Carter of the LCP regarding "two unhappy cases of coloured babies being born to two married women". Carter had forwarded the letter to Constantine, who wrote Miss Hillyer that he could not help as the proposed Home is still very far from completion".

8. Pastor Ekarte's request to Keith and Cummings to be on the Board is in Register of Correspondence PRO: C0977/5, file 11004/B4.
9. Constantine (see n.2), p.100. Unfortunately Constantine does not give a date for the winding up of the affairs of the committee.
10. Correspondence with Dr Kitty Fraser, December 1992 to September 1993. Dr Fraser, who had known Pastor Daniels since November 1941, described him as "a delightful man, a sincere Christian with a real love for children... A good, caring and loving man, doing what he believed to be right". She believes that the letters she has regarding the proposed home "show quite clearly that most of those involved were uneducated, ignorant and naive – which is just what Pastor Ekarte was himself... Ignorant in the sense of having very limited knowledge of what was going on and of what they were undertaking."
    I wish to thank Dr Fraser for writing to me and for sending me copies of some of the letters she had received from the Mission.
11. St. Clair Drake, 'Preliminary Statement' (see n.4), p.11.
12. Rhodes House Library: Br. Emp. Mss. s.23, Box H3/2.
13. *Australian Women's Weekly*, 19/7/1947; *Ebony* (an African-American weekly magazine based in Chicago), 197111946.
14. The 'news' about the "Brown Babies" was not carried in any other newspaper, as far as I have been able to ascertain. Regrettably Mr Kendall died some 10 years ago and his son has no knowledge of these events.
15. State Department, Washington to Embassy, London 15/4/1947, US National Archives: RG59/811.22/4-1547; Embassy to State 13/5/1947, RG59/ 811.2215-1347.
    As Dr Joseph-Mitchell has not left any papers, it has not been possible to determine whether he had any basis for casting such aspersions on either the Pastor or on Eddie DuPlan. Among the people I interviewed in Liverpool there was no consensus of opinion on DuPlan. No-one remembers him having a job, so we have to presume he 'lived by his wits'.
    Of Taylor nothing has been discovered. The Negro Welfare Centre has not been documented. After the war it still existed in some form as E.A Cowan, calling himself the 'General Secretary, Executive Committee, Negro Welfare Centres, Manchester', published a pamphlet, *A Call for Action!!*, n.d. (c.1949). (Fortuitously there was a copy of this rare pamphlet amongst Professor Kenneth Little's papers, to which access was kindly granted to me by the executor of his estate.) Nigerian-born Cowan went to teach trade unionists in the Gold Coast under Kwame Nkrumah's premiership. He returned to Nigeria after the overthrow of President Nkrumah in 1966.
16. Embassy to State Department 22/5/1947, US National Archives: RG59/ 811.2215-2247.
17. Embassy to State Dept 13/5/1947, US National Archives: RG59/811.2215-1347; Embassy to State 22/5/1947, US National Archives: RG59/811, 2215-2247.
18. It was estimated that in Germany there were some 7,000 illegitimate Black children; the Bavarian Ministry of Education reported 3,093 as being in school in October 1952. News releases Frankfurt 12/5/1959 and Munich 15/10/1952, Chicago Historical Library: Claude Barnett Papers, Box 198.

A 1952 survey in Germany reported that of these "mulatto children" 25% lived in orphanages or with foster parents. *Mental Hygiene*, July 1953. How difficult it was to arrive at the real numbers is demonstrated by a 1953 estimate of a total of 3,400 The Mission becomes a children's home, 1944-1949 children of mixed-parentage in Germany alone. *The Commonwealth*, 5/6/1953.

19. Embassy to State Dept 17/4/1947, US National Archives: RG591 811.22141747; Roy Wilkins to Margaret Halsey 26/4/1947, Library of Congress: NAACP Papers, Group II, A154.

For comments in the US press, see for example, *People's Voice*, 12, 19 & 26/4/1947.

One could perhaps ask whether Dr Moody's debunking was wholly in the quest for truth, as he was also trying to raise funds in the US. However, as the League's project was a cultural centre and no longer a home for children, perhaps there was no real conflict of interest, except that donors would be more likely to respond to a plea for children than for culture. Dr Moody received very few donations for his project in the US.

The Rainbow Home in Birkenhead, which had been supported by the League, was closed down in about August 1947 and the couple in charge, Mr & Mrs Russell, were prosecuted and fined for negligence. *Daily Mail* 3/9/1947, 17/9/1947, 23/10/1947; *Birkenhead News*, 3/8/1946; and George Padmore, 'Coloured Babies Perish in Hunger', *Ashanti Pioneer*, 1/11/1947, p.1. See also National Council for Voluntary Organisations Archives: Family Welfare Association, Information Sub-Committee meetings September 1946 to June 1947.

20. Walter White to George Padmore 17/4/1947, Padmore to White 29/4/1947, Library of Congress: NAACP Papers, Group II, A640 and J37.

In the US George Padmore was well known as a journalist contributing to the Black press. As a Marxist, Padmore would have been impressed by Pastor Daniels' work, not his Christianity, Though Padmore described DuPlan to White as having completed his legal studies, this is incorrect. According to the Keeper of Records of the Honourable Society of the Middle Temple, who I wrote me on 20/10/1992, he did not qualify as a barrister. [Note that DuPlan had been involved in the Mission in the 1930s. (See Chapter 4.)

21. See, for example, the *New York Amsterdam News*, 26/4/1947 and *Chicago Defender*, 3/5/1947.

22. *Chicago Defender*, 24/4/1948.

Whether Pastor Daniels ever attempted such an explanation, of class, poverty and racism in war damaged Britain, is not known. In May 1948 in a letter to Dr Fraser he claimed that Mrs Louis had offered him £250, which he told her to keep until a new building was found. She advised him to set up a committee and when he had done this she would establish a US board of trustees to collect funds.

23. *New York Amsterdam News*, 3 and 10/5/1947; *Chicago Defender* 3/5/1947. NCVO: Family Welfare Association, Information Sub-Committee Minutes for meeting on 19/3/1947.

24. Sylvia McNeill, *Illegitimate Children born in Britain to English Mothers and Coloured Americans*, League of Coloured People, nd (c.1945/46). See also Harold Moody, 'Anglo American Coloured Children' *The World's Children*, March 1946, pp.44-45.

Dr Harold Moody, the League of Coloured People's president, was a member of the committee of the Save the Children Fund (SCF). He raised the question of the children with the committee. This led to the SCF meeting with the Ministry of Health who declared that it was in consultation with the Home Office and the Colonial Office over the question of overseas adoptions. For the meeting Dr Moody had set up with the Ministry on February 19, the SCF agreed to send "independent observers without committing the Fund in any way".

Save the Children Fund: 100th Meeting of the Executive Committee 14/2/1946, #E. 1580.

25. Minutes of meetings and internal memorandum by Wilson 16/2/1946, PRO: F0371/5/617-AN3/3/45. "Putative" fathers who were not British subjects and who lived abroad were not permitted to adopt their own children. Home Office to Bow St. Police Court 7/1/1947, PRO: HO45/23127/82654/84.

26. *Hansard* 29/1/1947, cols. 208-9; 29/1/1948, col. 186 (written response).

27. St. Clair Drake reproduces the Pastor's letter of 28/10/1947 in his report to the Rosenwald Fund (see n. 1 above), p.12.

28. **I must here express my profound thanks to Mrs E. Revesz of the Department of Social Security's Departmental Record Office, who responded so readily to my request for information. All the material she sent me is cited as 'DSS'.**

The League of Coloured People's letter to the Ministry of Health 16/5/1945, DSS.

The first mention I have found of Pastor Daniels writing to the Colonial Office about the children is in Register of Correspondence PRO: C0977/3, file 11004/B4; in January 1945 he wrote thanking the Welfare Department for the usual £25 "subvention", but noted that he had not received anything extra for the children.

29. Report by Ms RW. Whiteway, 'Woman Inspector', 13/2/1946, DSS.

30. Report by Wainsborough Jones, 14/7/1946, DSS.

31. Report by R.W. Whiteway, 7/5/1946, DSS.

32. Reports of Dr Wright c.29/5/1947, PRO: HO45/24265/903260/3; 11/6/1948, PRO: H045/24265/903260/5.

33. Liverpool Society for the Prevention of Cruelty to Children to Home Office 14/5/1948, PRO: H045/24265/903260/3.

34. Dr Ruby Bell to the Colonial Office's Welfare Department 28/5/1948, Correspondence Register PRO: C0977/10, file 11030/7. The Register does not indicate if a reply was sent. The Pastor's pleas for a recommendation 19/7/1948 and 28/7/1948, in the same Register.

Dr Bell had founded Liverpool's Maternity and Child Welfare Department in 1919; she was appointed Senior Medical Officer in charge of Child Welfare in 1935.

35. Dr Wright to Mr Ekarte, undated draft of letter, PRO: H045/24265/903260/5.

36. Minutes by Dr Wright 21/6/1948; Dr Makepeace 29/6/ 1948; MacGregor 12/7/1948; Revell 14/2/1949, PRO: HO45/24265/903260/5.
37. The history of the closure of the home is put together from material in Home Office files PRO: HO45/24265/903260/3, 6, 7, 13, 14. The Home Office informed Mr Ekarte and also the Liverpool Town Clerk on 29/6/ 1949 that home was removed from the Register of Voluntary Homes. PRO: HO45/24265/903260/7.
38. Report from Liverpool Children's Department on visit to the Mount Olive Children's Home, 27/7/1949, PRO: HO45/24265/903260/13.
39. Minute by Under Secretary of State 11/7/1949, PRO: HO45/ 24265/903260/ 13.
40. See Graham Smith, *When Jim Crow Met John Bull*, I.B. Tauris, 1987. Chapter 8 deals with the general situation regarding the children fathered by African-American servicemen. Smith details the British government's attitude to the presence of Black servicemen and their children, which was often very racist.

CHAPTER SIX

Special events and visitors

Without the papers or even a full set of the annual reports of the Mission, it is possible to gain only a limited insight into the spectrum of special events or the full range of visitors to the Mission. Judging by the snippets of information available, it is evident that the Pastor held many special services and special events, partly to attract people (and funds) to the Mission, and also to bring some joy into the drab days of the 1930s. There were also meetings to discuss social issues.

Special Events

The information of the two special services described below comes from the pages of the weekly paper *West Africa*. Regrettably, it would appear that this journal banished Pastor Daniels from its pages at the end of 1935 when it passed into the ownership of Elder Dempster. The city's papers seldom carried news of the Mission, so it did not seem worthwhile to attempt the task of going through the pages of the three Liverpool papers.

At the service on the first Sunday in August 1934, while the International Anthropology Congress was meeting in Liverpool, the Pastor is reported as saying: "There are still too many people eager to discover the worst in us. My race, of which I am proud, has many good qualities, not least of which is the ability to think the best of those who so often think the worst of us... My people believe that the problems of the present and the future could be solved through careful and sympathetic study of the past." According to the *Daily Post* this Sunday was part of a series of special services to commemorate the abolition of slavery. Part of the Pastor's sermon was a description of the horrors of the trade in human beings.[1] Whether any of the academics at the Congress, some undoubtedly eugenicists, attended the service is not known.

At another of these thanksgiving services the congregation was addressed by Professor Wilberforce, the grandson of abolitionist William. The service was conducted by Pastor Daniels with the assistance of Revd Dr T.G. Campbell, a life governor of the British and Foreign Bible Society.[2]

The small pamphlet which was issued to celebrate emancipation was in two parts: the first re-told the history of slavery and emancipation. The second part was the story of the Pastor's own life. In the introduction to the history of slavery Pastor Daniels gives thanks to God for emancipation and prays for "justice to all mankind", and for relief and protection. "Negroes", he wrote, "whose proper and legitimate home was, and is, and ever shall be, Africa, but who are scattered and dispersed the world over, not by their wish, but by the woeful trick of circumstances that reveals a terrible history of the traffic in the bodies of men... We are a people who have already suffered most terribly from the greed, lust and viciousness and injustice of others of the human race, who have for centuries imposed upon us the horrors of slavery – chattel and industrial..."[3]

Just from these two surviving fragments of the Pastor's words we can begin to understand the power and passion, as well as the independent thought of Pastor Daniels, and why he was popular with so many of the Africans in Liverpool. We can also see why he became a suspect figure in some official and philanthropic circles. To call for justice and to speak of industrial slavery would have been seen as provocative. Then to evoke the ghost of Marcus Garvey's once powerful Universal Negro Improvement Association by calling his own endeavour the 'Universal Negro Improvement and African Churches Mission' indicates a fearless man who was clearly heading for collisions with authority.

That other special services were held is indicated in chapter 4. What is clear even from such fragments of evidence is that Pastor Daniels always mixed religion and politics.

It would appear that the Pastor was also determined to show that the Black peoples of Liverpool were as much part of (and as 'good' as) the city's population and/or any of the other ethnic groups. An example of this is the participation of the Mission's children in King George V's Silver Jubilee celebration. At the Youth March, "a round of applause greeted three small boys from the African Churches Mission when they gave their collection to the Lord Mayor" for the Jubilee Trust Fund. The church paper *Other Land*s described the Mission's Cubs, Guides and Scouts taking part in a Jubilee Rally. The Lord Mayor, who knew Pastor Daniels from a previous visit to the Mission, asked the Pastor to join him on the review platform.[4]

Visitors

The Mission, even from the few scattered pieces of evidence we have, received a constant flow of distinguished visitors. The 1933 report on the Mission mentions Melville Jones, Bishop of Lagos and A.B. Akinyele, the Assistant Bishop, as having stayed at the Mission. The Principal of Achimota College on the Gold Coast visited.[5]

In 1934 Mr G.T. Basden, Member for the Ibo Division of the Nigerian Legislative Council wrote in the Visitor's Book; "I inspected the premises and noted the use made of all the available space. Was interested to meet men from Ijaw, Calabar and Benin. From personal knowledge we shall be able to take more sympathetic interest in the work of the Mission."[6]

In 1937 Lt-Col J Sandeman Allen MP addressed a meeting on The Black and White Problem at the Mission and wrote in the Visitor's Book: "The African Churches Mission is doing very good work in the City".

The Revd A.C. Onyeabo, Assistant Bishop of the Diocese of Niger, visiting in July 1937, wrote in the Visitor's Book that he had "spent a good time with Pastor Ekarte who assisted me in getting round to see the important places and people of Liverpool. Revd Ekarte is doing a great deal of work among the coloured people and needs all the support that could be given to him." Among the people Pastor Daniels took the Assistant Bishop to see was the Lord Mayor of Liverpool.

The Bishop of the Niger Diocese, Revd B. Lasbrey, also visited and sent a copy of his pastoral letter describing the visit to the

Pastor. He had written: "We were very favourably impressed. It was entirely a surprise visit in the early afternoon... There was considerable activity even at that time of day... There is a big hall for services and meetings, rooms for classes, two or three bedrooms for strangers, club rooms and a canteen where men can get refreshment at a cheap rate. We saw several young men in the club room, one or two amongst whom were Ibos. We examined the various registers and books which were tidily and cleanly kept... Mr.Ekarte visits ships coming from West Africa to welcome African visitors and others and to try to look after them while they are on shore."

These excerpts from the Bishop's pastoral letter were re printed in a 4-page magazine Pastor Daniels had started, called *Black and White*. The first issue is dated October-December 1933; no other issues have been found.[7]

Among other visitors in 1937 were Ademola III, the Alake (King) of Abeokuta (Nigeria) and the Senior Resident (British Administrator) at Abeokuta, Mr A.E. Murray. After an address of welcome by Mr E.A. Mensah, the Mission's Secretary, the Alake toured the Mission and promised financial assistance.[8]

Very sadly, the Visitor's Book has been lost. Without it we shall never know the full range of celebrities who visited and commended the Mission. Paul Robeson certainly visited, as had Joe Louis and his wife. (On Mrs Louis's visit see chapter 5.) Of the many men who became famous later in life, Jomo Kenyatta, Dr Hastings Banda and Kwame Nkrumah (first prime ministers of independent Kenya, Malawi and Ghana respectively) had stayed at the Mission.[9] A regular annual visitor was Prince Monolulu, the then well-known racing tipster.[10]

Naturally, during the war the number of distinguished guests and visitors declined. Lord Leverhulme visited; also Sir Arthur Bromley and Oliver Stanley, the Secretary of State for the Colonies, in February 1943. Some of the members of the National Council of Nigeria and the Cameroons visited in 1942 and the Nigerian Press Delegation in 1943; both were led by Dr Nnamdi Azikiwe, who was to become independent Nigeria's Governor-General.[11]

Some of the Mission's neighbours remember important visitors coming. One name mentioned was that of George Padmore, the Pan-Africanist. Undoubtedly Ras T. Makonnen, Padmore's Manchester-based colleague had been there many times. This must also be true of Learie Constantine, as all three had been involved with fundraising for the proposed Booker T. Washington Home.

NOTES AND REFERENCES

1. *West Africa*, 18/8/1934; *Liverpool Daily Post* 6/8/1934. The service was addressed by Mr G.O. Ganton; *West Africa*, 4/8/1934.
2. *West Africa*, 20/10/1934.
3. *The African Churches Mission*, n.d, pamphlet, Rhodes House Library: Br. Emp. Mss. s.23, Box H1/21. There is also a typescript in Box H1/20.
4. *Liverpool Daily Post*, 13/5/1935; *Other Lands*, January 1936, Pp.79-80.
5. The African Churches Mission, August 1933, Rhodes House Library: Br. Emp. Mss, s.23, Box H1/21.
6. List of visitors and their comments from *The African Churches Mission and Training Home*, undated pamphlet (c.1938), Schomburg Research Center, New York; Phelps Stokes Papers. (These papers were unsorted when I had access to them.)
7. *Black and White*, No.1, October-December 1933, Rhodes House Library: Br. Emp. Mss. s.23, Box H1/21.
8. *Evening Express*, 9/7/1937; *The African Churches Mission and Training Home*, c.1938 (see n.6), p.8.
9. Interviews as previously noted; *Flamingo*, August 1934, pp.11-12.
10. On Prince Monolulu, see his *I Gotta Horse*, Hurst & Blackett, London, n.d.
11. Rear Admiral (later Sir) Arthur Bromley was the Private Secretary (Ceremonial and Reception) to the Secretary of State for the Colonies; Lord Leverhulme was the governor (chairman) of Lever Bros. and Unilever Ltd., the largest British trading company in West Africa. He was Pro-Chancellor of the University of Liverpool 1932-36.

CHAPTER SEVEN

The Mission's relationship with other organisations

Black Organisations

Besides the Mission, there were two other Black associations in Liverpool in the 1930s. One was the Gold Coast Aborigines Club, founded in 1932, whose secretary in 1936 was J. Sam Kojo-Asare. The other was the Native Union of Empire Africans founded in 1935 by A.K. Kpakpa Quartey, which protested against the invasion of Abyssinia by Italy. The activities of these organisations and their relationship to the African Churches Mission is unknown.[1]

Pastor Daniels was known to Black organisations outside Liverpool. For example, in August 1937, after attending a convention in south Wales, he "called at Cardiff to visit the thousands of my people there and was very much appalled with what greeted me in one of the streets of their locality: there, on the street, were men busily engaged in gambling, e.g., shooting dice and playing cards... If some of the organised bodies in this Christian country who send Missionaries to Africa will help us in instituting a branch of the African Churches Mission and Training Home in Cardiff, I am sure the men will have enough to occupy their time other than shooting dice in the streets." This hope was never realised.[2]

The League of Coloured People's journal, *The Keys*, first mentioned the Pastor in its October-December 1934 issue, when he was among the speakers at the League's conference, 'The Negro in the World Today'. (See chapter 4.) *The Keys* carried a brief half-page article by the Pastor describing the work of the Mission in July-September 1936.

Though he could not attend the League's 1937 General Conference, Pastor Daniels sent a telegram of good wishes. The issue of *The Keys* which noted this also printed a photograph of Rev. G. Daniels Ekarte on the back page. The caption states that he has done "invaluable work" and that the League had "decided to develop his work and give him full support... Mr. Ekarte is trying to rejuvenate the branch of the League founded in Liverpool some years ago". This paternalistic and somewhat contradictory statement reveals much about the League's attitudes. These sentiments were repeated a few years later, when League representatives attended the Mission's 11th Anniversary services. In its brief report of the event, the League noted that the Pastor had been working in his own way on behalf of his people consistently for 20 years... He is now regarded by one and all as an outstanding man in Liverpool and his work deserves all the support that can be given thereto." A few months previously the League had advised the readers of its *Newsletter* that the Pastor "catered for seamen... His influence is most beneficial... He faces many difficulties; the greatest are financial, and the problem of justifying himself and his work to the local authorities... We admire his persistence and wish him well."[3]

When this original branch of the League had been established in Liverpool, and whether Pastor Daniels did anything to resuscitate it, is unknown. However, a branch was certainly established in July 1942. Its president was Dr Hastings Banda. "Dr Banda, who became the first president of independent Malawi, had stayed at the Mission when he first arrived in Liverpool to set up his medical practice in St. James Place, a stone's throw from Hill Street. The secretary was Dr R. Wellesley Cole, a Sierra Leonean physician practising in Newcastle, and its vice-president was Mr Forbes Christian. Pastor Daniels represented "coloured" Liverpudlians at the inaugural meeting on July 11th.[4]

Because of the problems in Liverpool arising from of the presence of large numbers of Black and White American troops near the city, the League' president, Dr Harold Moody, visited Liverpool in November 1942. He found that the West Indian "technicians"of war service in the Liverpool area were not having their needs met and that the Black population's problems with housing and education, and employment for the children were being ignored. Dr Moody set up a series of meetings with the Bishop and various philanthropic organisations. A committee, chaired by the Bishop and composed of the city's philanthropic and religious elite, was soon established to raise funds for a social centre. Pastor Daniels was not on this committee, though Dr Moody noted at the end of the year that the League was "relying on Pastor Daniel Ekarte's expert knowledge, advice and direction."[5] One can only presume that this was cold comfort for the Pastor.

Pastor Daniels and the Mission were well known to Ras T. Makonnen, the Pan-African activist and restaurant-owner in Manchester. Makonnen described the Pastor in his book *Pan-Africanism from Within*: "Ekarte found a need among the African seamen, and gradually created a little world for himself by building up this little shanty sort of building for seamen in the slums of Liverpool. It's difficult to analyse the role of such welfare workers; some would say that they tend to magnify the suffering of their people and create a bureaucracy to deal with it. And certainly a number of white seamen were suspicious of the power base a man like Ekarte could build up against unity. Ekarte was opposed to unionisation because he had his own way of dealing with Africans' needs. Despite this, a man like Ekarte could make himself indispensable by his ability to deal with West African languages, and even the more class-conscious people like Dorothy Woodman and Nancy Cunard were therefore tolerant of Ekarte and felt: We have a good man in Liverpool who is helping to solve the problems of the coloured fellows."[6] What the socialist Makonnen ignores in this assessment is that the National Union of Seamen was hostile to Black seamen. The Pastor had definitely not created a bureaucracy, but a social centre to which all those in need could turn.

Pastor Daniels was appreciated by the political activists who attended the Pan-African Congress in Manchester in 1945. Though the Pastor is not listed as attending the Congress, one of the resolutions called for continued support for the Mission amongst other African associations, and asked for "assistance by the responsible authorities to continue their vital social work."[7]

Pastor Daniels must have known, and been known by, other political figures in the UK. For example an entry dated February 1941 in the Mission Ledger is a list of contacts given by the Pastor to the Revd Laminah Sankoh. The list includes Padmore, Ladipo Solanke of the West African Students Union, the left-wing scholar J.R. Horrabin and the head of the National Council of Labour Colleges, Mr J. Millar. A brief note from Solanke to Pastor Daniels in September 1943, in which Solanke refuses an invitation due to a prior engagement, indicates that the two men kept in touch.[8]

Local organisations

The African Churches Mission does not appear in any listing of Liverpool social and seamen's welfare organisations. (It should also be noted that there is no mention at all of Liverpool's 'coloured' population in the Liverpool Council of Social Service's journal, *Liverpool Quarterly*, for the years 1932-1939. Nor, for that matter, in the civic-oriented *Liverpolitan*.)

With the Association for the Welfare of Half-Caste Children, Pastor Daniels' relationship must have been somewhat less than cordial, if one is to judge from Harold King's comments on the Pastor: "One or two people in Liverpool who know him well think him an extremely dangerous person... He is plausible – and I'm sorry that he seems to have won the complete confidence of Collet's organisation" (the League of Coloured People).[9]

In 1938 the Association reorganised itself and, after protests from the League about the term 'half-caste' renamed itself the Association for the Welfare of Coloured People. (It is likely, of course, that the Pastor and others had also protested, but if they had, the Association had not valued their advice.) In 1939 Harold King resigned, and a man seemingly of less racist attitudes, Ian McLuckie, replaced him as Warden of the University Settlement and hence the main worker in the Association. There is a slight indication of an improved relationship between the Mission and the Association in that girls from the Mission were invited to dances the Association had organised for Black US servicemen. Apparently no other girls had been invited: did the Association hold segregated dances?[10]

Relations with religious bodies

When the Mission was opened the Pastor had a number of supporters from the Christian churches. These included Liverpool's Bishop and Canon Davey of the Cathedral.

However, in 1937 something occurred which for a while distanced the Bishop from the Mission. The events are unclear, but it seems that the Pastor was accused of financial irregularities. The police were involved, but as the Liverpool Council of Social Service wrote to John Harris, "no-one thinks that the police action was justified".[11]

By the following year relations had been restored. In reply to a Colonial Office enquiry about the Pastor, the Bishop replied that "the African Churches Mission has been carried on for many years by Daniels Ekarte, who has done some really good work. But he is less than a child in finance, and has made a hopeless mess of that side of the mission. I'm trying to get two or three laymen to look after its financial affairs, and I think that if we can get over some present difficulties the Mission will be on a sound basis. If you are in touch with any source of help...it would be better to send contributions to me. I will see that they are properly used..."[12] The one Mission Ledger in existence bears out the Bishop's allegation about record-keeping being a 'mess'. Whether the Pastor would have welcomed donations going to the Bishop, and the Bishop determining expenditure, is questionable.

How this proposed intervention by the Bishop was resolved is not known. By the 1940s relations must have been amicable as in 1943 the Pastor served on the Bishop's committee mentioned above. As Dr Moody did not list the Pastor as a member, had the Bishop put him on the committee?[13]

Relations between the coloured population and the churches were apparently not always free from the racism endemic in British society. For example, St. Saviour's Church in 1926 had referred to the Black children in its chair as the "coon quartet". During World War II a church in Birkenhead excluded West Indians. Others claim that they were not welcome at the local Roman Catholic church, whose priest told them to worship at the Mission. An African student studying in Manchester in the mid-1940s tried to attend a service in a Liverpool church and was also told to leave and go to the African mission.[14]

However, by the late 1940s, Mr Daniels appears to have had cordial relations with at least some of the local churches. The Mission's "young people" paid visits to St. Mary's Church, Wavertree; Allerton Presbyterian Church; Formby Methodist Church; Walton Baptist Church, Orrell Park, and Hamilton Church.[15] Having been raised on a mission station, Pastor Daniels might have had a special interest in missionary work, but the only evidence of this is a brief mention that the Pastor had attended a missionary meeting at the Highfield Congregational Church, Rock Ferry, (nr. Liverpool) in November 1934. He is reported as saying that "the English are kind, lovable and considerate".[16]

Relations with the Colonial Office

In the first half of the 20th century, people of African descent living permanently or temporarily in the UK were not the responsibility of any government departments. No ministry was concerned or interested in the racial discrimination met by Black people in almost all areas of their lives. If a Black dignitary met racial discrimination, for example at the hands of hoteliers, a question might be asked in Parliament. The responsible Minister would loudly proclaim how much he deplored such behaviour, against which legislation was, of course, inappropriate. About the only time the Colonial Office and/or the Home Office became involved was when questions of deportation arose. Until the late 1940s it was the Aliens branch of the Home Office that dealt with 'coloured' people, even though the majority were British subjects.

When there were any problems which came to the notice of the public, it was generally thought that the Colonial Office should deal with it as the people involved were 'obviously' from the colonies. This was not true: there were Black peoples born in the UK, and others, such as Black Americans and Africans and people of African descent not from British colonies, who were also in the UK. The interests of the Colonial Office were to govern the colonies and to ensure that no events concerning Black peoples in the UK should fuel anti-British sentiment in the empire.

Though the suggestion was made in 1937, the Colonial Office did not establish a Welfare Department until the outbreak of World War II. The war saw the arrival of people of African descent from everywhere in the empire: they came, or were brought by the British government, to work in munitions and other factories and in forestry; to man the merchant navy and to serve in the armed forces.[17] The Welfare Department had been given responsibility for all these special arrivals, as well as the resident Black population and the colonial students. The Department liaised with other government ministries such as Health and Labour, the Air Force and the Army over pertinent issues. It visited places of employment, cajoled recalcitrant and racist officials in unions, factories, local government, etc., and set up a Welfare Committee in 1943, which included some Black members. Once it had obtained a budget, the Department grant-aided Black organisations and funded community centres as well as student and seamen's hostels. Though the Department's mandate was the many aspects of the welfare of colonial peoples in the UK, its prime consideration had to be the retention of the empire's loyalty, especially in time of war. It was believed that any information regarding incidents of racial discrimination reaching the empire could undermine this loyalty. For this reason news to the colonies was heavily censored and colonial newspapers were tightly controlled. Nevertheless, un-censored news did reach the colonies through the merchant seamen, even if it could not be printed.[18]

It appears that the first time Pastor Daniels contacted the Colonial Office was in 1936; on 4 September he wrote that "the entire half-caste population is unemployed", and had no chance of getting jobs. What was required was technical education for the children. Could the Colonial Office help? The CO replied that it could not help with educational matters and advised the Pastor to approach the Liverpool Education Department. In an internal memo, W.J. Bigg noted that "the objects of the Mission are very praiseworthy, but we have no funds to help them." [19]

It has not been possible to discover whether Pastor Daniels did get in touch with the Education Department. However, even if he had, clearly nothing or very little was done. The League of Coloured People reported in January 1943 that only a "handful of Black children have attended the secondary and technical schools." Black youngsters were excluded from the Department's youth centres.[20] If we use the Pastor's dream of coaching children for the scholarship examination and setting up a technical college as evidence, it is safe to say that Black children continued to be under-educated. The first known admission of a Black child to the elite grammar schools (academic high schools) was not until the 1960s.

The Mission's correspondence with the Colonial Office for 1937 has not been preserved, but we know he wrote again, asking for funds. The CO, as in 1936, replied that it had no funds. Pastor Daniels then asked for suggestions for possible sources of funds. This resulted in the Colonial Office asking the Home Office for its opinion about aid from government funds. The Home Office's Aliens Department's reply avoided the question, Ms Wall wrote promising information on the Mission soon. If this was ever sent, it has not been preserved. From whom would the Home Office have obtained information? The local police? The Immigration Office?[21]

In 1941 both officers of the new Welfare Department visited and reported favourably on the Mission. Mr Ivor Cummings, of Sierra Leone descent, reported that "it is clear that Mr. Ekarte is the bridgehead of the Africans in Liverpool; in addition he is closely in touch with those born in Liverpool and he visits them in their homes and talks with their parents... I believe that we shall find Mr. Ekarte and his organisation most useful, and I hope we shall make full use of it." During this visit Mr Cummings discussed with the Pastor "the difficulties which have arisen between Africans and the West Indians who are working in Ordnance factories," and also the strengthening of the Mission's Committee by asking Mr Paul to return.

Despite this strong recommendation from his junior, Mr J.L. Keith wrote to Paul that though he had "every sympathy for Ekarte's work and will encourage it, it would not be wise to build on his organisation." (Paul was at this time a Port Welfare Officer.)

Unaware of this, Pastor Daniels wrote to Mr Cummings arguing that his own desire to extend the work of the Mission and Mr Cummings's desire to extend facilities in Liverpool coincided. The needs were for a club, a hostel, and for "spiritual work." Either a larger building was required, or at a renovated Mission, he could continue the spiritual work, while a paid secretary ran the club. The hostel should be a separate building. Could the Colonial Office refurbish the Mission building?[22] Nothing came of this suggestion.

Nevertheless, the Welfare Department appears to have maintained close contact with Pastor Daniels and to have used his knowledge of Liverpool as guidance in its deliberations. For example, in July 1942, when West Africans working in the munitions factories were being discussed, Mr Cummings mentioned that the Pastor had told him that as there was no opportunity to aid the war effort at home, West Africans, especially Nigerians, were coming to Britain to work in the factories. West African ex-seamen were also working in local factories.[23]

In October 1942 the Colonial Office set up the Advisory Committee for the Welfare of Colonial People in the UK and appointed Drs Moody and Wellesley Cole as members. At the very first meeting of this Committee, a special paper on the Mission advised members that the Pastor "had been doing a certain amount of welfare work amongst the large community of seamen who have been neglected in the past in so far as no satisfactory provision was made for their welfare."[24]

As few other Colonial Office files have survived, all that is known of the subsequent relationship is that in 1941 the Colonial Office began, and then continued, to give some financial support to the Mission. (See chapter 8) During the 'Brown Babies' crisis, the Colonial Office was sympathetic, but took no steps to help Pastor Daniels. In 1948, according to a CO Register of Correspondence, the Pastor asked the Colonial Office for old army clothes for stowaways. The Register does not note a response. From 1950 Pastor Daniels vanishes even from the pages of the Colonial Office registers.

Relations with local government

There is not one mention of the Pastor or the Mission in the Minutes of Liverpool's civic committees.

In 1937, after her visit to the Mission, Ethel Fegan of Girton College approached the Under Secretary of State at the Colonial Office. Pastor Daniels, she wrote, is "recognised as useful by City Authorities such as the police who send coloured men to him and appeal to him if any coloured man is in trouble. Both the Mayor and the Bishop could tell you about him. I looked over his house. His pride in it was pathetic, as were the obvious signs of poverty. There are just about the barest necessities in it. I think some of his difficulty may be due to natural ignorance of the best way of running things in this country, and he said, rather wistfully, that in Nigeria one could always go to a Resident for help and advice, but here there seems to be no-one. Is this true, and is there a Department of the Colonial Office that could advise him?"[25]

From April 1933 the Pastor's Ledger provides evidence of men being referred to the Mission by the police. The Ledger seldom states why the person was being referred, only what help was given. However, by 1941 the Pastor's relationship with the police had apparently deteriorated. In his report of his visit to the Mission in October, Mr Cummings noted that "in his struggle to obtain a square deal for the African seaman he has also incurred the displeasure of the Police; although they make no specific charges against Mr.Ekarte, they seem to doubt his moral rectitude... I have had one or two talks with the Police concerning the Pastor and I believe my contact with them has changed their attitudes." (It should be remembered that the previous year the Pastor had campaigned for an increase in the pay of West African seamen.)[26]

The city's Immigration Officer also used the Mission as a place to send stowaways. As demonstrated in the context of the adopted children, the hospitals and local agencies consulted the Pastor about the placement of these children.

Relations with the American military

It is not known how or when Pastor Daniels established relations with the US military authorities. Undoubtedly some African American troops on leave in Liverpool soon found their way to the Mission.

By the Christmas of 1943 Major Taafel was photographed at the Mission with the toys donated to the Mission children by the US Army.[27] Many people who lived in the area at the time recall that the Mission received food and toys from the military.

In June 1944 when there were disturbances involving US troops in Liverpool, General Lee and Pastor Daniels corresponded about the situation. Some nine months later the Headquarters of the US military asked the Commanding Officer of the Western District for information on the "Home for Coloured Children".[28]

NOTES AND REFERENCES

1. *West Africa*, 27/6/1936, 30/11/1935; *Liverpool Daily Post*, 4/12/1945.
2. *The African Churches Mission and Training Home,* pamphlet n.d. (c.1938), Schomburg Research Center: Phelps Stokes Papers. On Black organisations in Cardiff, see Marika Sherwood, 'Racism and Resistance: Cardiff in the 1930s and 1940s', *Llafur,* 5/4, 1991.
3. League of Coloured People's *Newsletter,* August 1942, pp.102-3; May 1942, p.45.
4. I have not been able to discover anything about Mr Christian. See Robert Wellesley Cole, *An Innocent in Britain*, Campbell Matthews, London, 1988; *Newsletter,* August 1942, p.110.
5. *Newsletter,* October 1942, p.5; November, p.60; December, p.71; March 1943, p.163.
6. Ras T. Makonnen, *Pan-Africanism from Within*, recorded and edited by Kenneth King, Oxford University Press, 1973, p. 130. (Makonnen was born Peter Griffiths in British Guiana.) I have augmented the text from the transcripts of the original tape-recordings from which this book is edited. (The tapes are in the possession of the editor, Dr K. King, Edinburgh University.) Makonnen's commercial enterprises financed the Pan-African movement, and other Black political enterprises.

    Dorothy Woodman was a socialist, at one time secretary of the Women's International League, and became secretary of the Union of Democratic Control. She was the life-long companion of Kingsley Martin, the editor of the *New Stateman and Nation* when it was a socialist weekly. Nancy Cunard, born into a minor branch of the millionaire shipping family, was a journalist and publisher. She worked for a while with George Padmore and was an accepted person in Black socialist circles in the UK. There is an unsatisfactory biography of her by Anne Chisholm (Penguin, 1981), which does not deal adequately with her Black and political involvements. Nancy Cunard's most famous publication is a 700 page anthology of Black Relationship with other organisations and African literature, poetry, history and art, *Negro*, published in 1934. A much-abridged version is available in paperback, published by Frederick Ungar Publishing Co., New York, 1970.

7. George Padmore, *Pan-Africanism or Communism* (1956), Anchor Books, 1972, pp.140-141.
8. Ladipo Solanke to Daniels Ekarte 30/9/1943, Lagos University; WASU Papers, Solanke Correspondence, Box 72. Since I saw these papers they have been re-sorted and hence this box number is probably incorrect.
9. Harold King to John Harris of the Anti-Slavery Society 29/10/1937, Rhodes House Library: Br. Emp. Mss. s.23, H1/21. Harold King was the warden of the University Settlement, which was the parent body of the Association for the Welfare of Half-Caste Children.
10. Liverpool University: Minutes of Settlement Council for 27 October 1942.
    War-time segregation in Liverpool and elsewhere in the UK was not uncommon; for example, it was admitted in Parliament that at the Allied Centre in Liverpool, run by the British Council, private rooms were "reserved for particular nationalities". *Hansard*, 17/12/1942, col. 2115. A Liverpool cinema displayed a sign "No Coloured Allowed" in 1943. *Newsletter*, March 1943, pp.174-5. See also Janet Toole, 'GIs and the Race Bar in Wartime Warrington', *History Today*, July 1993, pp.22–28.
11. Charity Organisation Society to John Harris 30/12/1937, enclosing letter from L Redfearn, Assistant Secretary, Liverpool Council of Social Service 22/12/1937, Rhodes House Library: Mss. Br. Emp. 5.23, H1/25.
12. Hanns Vischer, Colonial Office to the Bishop of Liverpool 27/4/1938 and the Bishop's reply 28/4/1938, PRO: C0847/11/5. Vischer's status in the Colonial Office is unclear. Some suspect him of having been an intelligence officer.
    That matters had been cleared up did not prevent the weekly paper John Bull (4/6/1938, p.15) from alleging that the Pastor had "confiscated" funds. The paper demanded that he should be "cleared out."
13. J.L. Keith of the Colonial Office to Mr Chance, Treasury, 28/7/1943, PRO: C0876/38 (11004869).
    The Liverpool Diocesan Registry was bombed in 1941 "and many papers lost forever"; the Bishop assured me that there are no materials regarding the Mission remaining there. However, as the Diocesan Registrar told me that non-Church of England files have not been sorted out and indexed I requested permission to search the Registry holdings. This was not granted. (The Bishop suggested that his predecessor may have acted in his private capacity. This was not so – *vide* his interaction with the Colonial Office.
14. Interview with Mrs Higgins-Weaver, et al, in Carlton Wilson, A Hidden History: The Black Experience in Liverpool, England, 1919-1945, PhD Dissertation, University of North Carolina at Chapel Hill 1992, p.380; Anthony Richmond, *Colour Prejudice in Britain*, Routledge & Kegan Paul

1954, p.96; Eyo Bassey Ndem, Negro Immigrants in Manchester, MA Thesis, University of London 1953, p.233.

15. These visits are listed in *The African Churches Mission and Training Home*, pamphlet, n.d (c.1947/1948) p. 7, PRO: H045/24265. It is not known if such visits were a new venture.

16. *West Africa*, 1/12/1934.

17. On some aspects of the history of workers from the West Indies brought to Britain during the war, and the colour bar in the armed services, see Marika Sherwood, *Many Struggles*, Karia Press, London, 1985.

18. The work of the Colonial Office's Welfare Department has not been documented.

19. Daniels Ekarte to the Secretary of State for the Colonies 4/9/1936; reply 17/9/1936 and another, n.d.; minute by W.J. Bigg 11/9/1936, PRO: CO323/1407/4.

20. League of Coloured People, *Report on the Social Conditions of Liverpool's Coloured Population*, n.d. (sent by the League to the Colonial Office on 2/1/1943), PRO: C0876/36 (11004/42).

21. J.E.W. Flood of the Colonial Office to the Under Secretary of State at the Home Office 7/10/1937; Ms J.I. Wall (HO) to the Under Secretary of State at the Colonial Office 29/10/1937, PRO: CO323/1521. The question of establishing a welfare department is discussed in the minutes of this file.

22. Daniels Ekarte to Ivor Cummings 19/11/1941, PRO: C0859/76/10.

23. Memorandum from Ivor Cummings to J.L. Keith 23/7/1942, PRO: CO876/44.

24. Paper 7 for the first meeting of the Advisory Committee for the welfare of Coloured People in the UK, 2/10/1942, in the author's possession. This, together with some other papers of the Committee, was given to me by Mr Ivor Cummings in 1979, Mr Cummings died in 1992.

25. Ethel Fegan to Sir John Maffey 24/6/1937, PRO: CO323/1521/2.

26. Report by Ivor Cummings on his visit to Liverpool, 6/10/1941, PRO: C0859776/10.

27. *Liverpool Daily Post*, 22/12/1943.

28. US National Archives: RG332/291.2 'Negroes'– list of files destroyed 1943-1944, General Lee to Daniels Ekarte 9/6/1944, 17/6/1944; RG332/005 Gifts and Charities Vol. 1 1944 – list of papers destroyed, HQ, UK base ETOUSA to Commanding Officer Western District, 18/3/1945.

CHAPTER EIGHT

The financial struggle

The life of the Mission was a constant struggle for survival. This was the fate of all Black-led organisations. Even Dr Harold Moody's League of Coloured People, whose leading members were from the Black professional middle class, and which always strove for acceptance by similar White philanthropic organisations, often fell on hard times. Without the income from fundraising events and from its relatively affluent Black supporters, the League could not have survived. Pastor Daniels, though well-known in Liverpool and elsewhere, could not attract such support. Neither could he raise funds from his parishioners, many of whose incomes must have been at the barest subsistence level, at least in the 1930s.

In June 1931, when the Mission was opened, donations paid for the year's lease (£80) for 122-124 Hill Street. By 1937 the rent was £90 annually and, according to Ethel Fegan, "the Pastor's people are too poor to be able to help much." How was the Mission to keep paying the rent and to finance its activities? Heating, rates, electricity, fares, postage, meals, gowns for the choir as well as the Pastor's and the housekeeper's necessities all had to be paid for. The total expenditure for 1933 was £260.[1]

At the August 1933 commemoration and thanksgiving for Emancipation, the Pastor announced that he was launching an appeal for £5,000. Donations would be received by the Chairman, Revd Shields, the Treasurer, Revd Wilkie, or any of the Mission's four secretaries. In his newsletter *Black and White*, the Pastor acknowledges local donations of just over £30, and a "substantial subscription from the Niger Diocese." The indication is that the average annual donation from local sources was about £120.

At about this time the Mission issued a fundraising postcard which depicted the Pastor with the Revd Thomas G. Campbell, a life governor of the British and Foreign Bible Society, who had been a missionary in Nigeria. There is also another postcard, of the Pastor alone.[2]

The Anti-Slavery Society

The appeal was not very successful, so in 1934 the Pastor approached the Anti-Slavery Society for funds. This Society, besides conducting a continuous campaign against all forms of slavery, had some funds which it could use to aid Black peoples in Britain. Its secretary at this time, John Harris (later Sir John) suffered from the common British disease of racism, of the paternalistic variety. In April 1934 Pastor Daniels explained to Harris that the freehold of his premises had been offered to him for £1,300. Being a West African, "not many sources of borrowing are open to me," he wrote. Could the Society give him a loan to buy the house? It could either be put in the name of the Society with the Mission remaining as tenant, or in the name of the Mission's trustees, who could repay the loan at the rate of £78 annually. A further £500 was required to build an annex in the backyard. The brusque reply from Harris advised the Pastor to arrange a mortgage through a solicitor. Harris thus totally ignored the reason why Pastor Daniels had made the proposition in the first place: that Black people found it very difficult to get a mortgage. (A situation all too familiar 60 years later!)[3]

Despite repeated requests, the Anti-Slavery Society never gave Pastor Daniels a penny. This is not surprising as the Pastor's adamant belief in equality would have been anathema to the supremacist ideology of John Harris.[4]

After Sir John's death in 1940, relations improved between the Mission and the Society, which was now under the leadership of Barbadian-born C.W.W. Greenidge. Between October 1945 and August 1947 the Society sent a total of £25 to Pastor Daniels. Greenidge also agreed to become a patron of the proposed Booker T. Washington Children's Home. From 1948 until at least 1956 the Society sent an annual donation of £5. In September 1949

Greenidge promised to mention the Mission's needs to others as the Society could not increase its contribution.[5]

Towards the end of 1937, perhaps due to rumours of financial chicanery mentioned in chapter 7, the Mission was very hard pressed for funds. Pastor Daniels had to seek help even from those who had no sympathy for his work: in October he asked Warden Harold King of the University Settlement to make a donation to the Mission. King, a protégé of John Harris, naturally refused.[6]

Institute of African Languages and Culture

In April 1938, having failed with the Anti-Slavery Society and the Colonial Office (see below), the Pastor turned to the enigmatic figure of Hanns Vischer, director of the Institute of African Languages and Culture, Vischer was closely linked to the Colonial Office, but in what precise capacity remains obscure. Vischer asked the Bishop of Liverpool for information. On receiving a favourable reply (see previous chapter), Vischer wrote to philanthropist Lady Kathleen Simon recommending support for the Mission.[7]

In September the Pastor wrote again to Vischer, saying that the landlords were threatening to evict him. Evidently Lady Simon had not helped. As she was a member of the Anti-Slavery Society, she may well have been influenced against the Mission by Harris.

The anonymous donors' largesse

However, Pastor Daniels was not evicted. An anonymous donor (or donors) gave him sufficient money to buy the Mission building. Of all the people associated with the Mission, it has been suggested to me that the donor was either a Mrs Campbell of the Lancashire and Cheshire Rubber Company, or a Mrs M.B. Carr, who was one of the four secretaries of the Mission in 1933. An unnamed correspondent of the present Bishop states that the funds came from Mrs Carr and from an unknown source in Aberdeen.[8]

In 1939 the Synod of the Diocese of Niger voted to send £25 to the Mission. In 1945 the government of Nigeria also approved a grant, for an unknown sum. In 1948 the Gold Coast government asked the Colonial Office for information on the Mission as the Pastor had sent numerous requests for funds.

The Colonial Office

In December 1937 a Colonial Office official noted that the Pastor "has approached us a number of times," but had always been refused. Pastor Daniels sent a printed appeal in 1937, which showed that his expenditure for 1936 had been £892 which included £238 for free meals.[9]

Some Colonial Office officials were not unsympathetic: for example, Mr Sidebottom commented that the Mission was "probably a deserving case". Mr Williams felt the Mission was "probably more deserving than the West African Students Union – I feel rather sorry". But all the Colonial Office gave Pastor Daniels was sympathy; it would not even recommend his appeal to the West African governments.[10]

Another appeal, which the Pastor must have addressed to the League of Coloured People, was forwarded to the Colonial Office, who in turn sent it on to John Harris. Harris replied that the Pastor was a "vigorous beggar" whom the Anti-Slavery Society had already refused to aid.[11]

In January 1938, the Pastor tried again, explaining that the Mission was threatened with "extinction". He added that the Mission was the only "organisation in the country which caters for Africans and their children". He wrote again in June, stating that the Mission's debts were £500. In September he sent the balance sheets for 1937, and again asked for support. To each request the Colonial Office responded with sympathy, but no money.[12]

The Colonial Office's files on the Mission for 1939 and 1940 are missing. In 1941, the Welfare Department having been established, the Senior Welfare Officer visited the Mission. J.L. Keith called in July. He reported that the Mission was "lacking amenities, but was scrupulously clean... Gained impression that Ekarte does admirable work, deserving of support."[13]

In November 1941 the Ministry of Labour appointed a new Port Welfare Officer to Liverpool. Mr R.B. Paul, the ex Managing Director of West African Newspapers Ltd, was more sympathetic and familiar with West Africans than the previous Welfare Officer. He was also familiar with the Mission, having at one time been its Treasurer. (It is possible that he still was, or was again, in that office.) His reports of the Mission were favourable, as were those of Ivor Cummings. Mr Cummings set about getting some practical help for the Mission: for example, in October he asked the British Council to supply the Mission with papers and periodicals. Some financial aid was also made available: in December Mr Keith sent Paul £25 "for the West Africans and Ekarte." Four days later he sent £5 directly to the Pastor, with a letter stating that the Colonial Office was examining the question of better club and hostel facilities in Liverpool; Keith hoped to be able to discuss this with Pastor Daniels early in 1942.[14]

Information for 1942 is far more sparse. In August the Colonial Office sent another £25 to the Mission via Mr Paul and £10 for the children's Christmas party. In October the Pastor travelled to London for an interview at the Colonial Office.[15]

Presumably as a result of this interview, the following year Keith recommended to the Treasury that the Mission should be given a grant of £75 – and that it might be "politic to continue supporting the Mission's social and religious work" even after the Treasury-financed community centre was opened. The Treasury granted the £75.[16]

The files for 1943, 1944 and 1945 have also been destroyed. The Colonial Office sent a grant in 1943 and 1944, but the amount is unknown. The grant for 1945 was £25, which was the first instalment of an annual grant approved for five years. In 1946 Pastor Daniels requested a loan of £200, but the Correspondence Register does not indicate what the response was. It appears that in 1950 both the Colonial Office and the Nigerian government terminated their grants.[17]

The £75 and the other grants from the Colonial Office, plus the £125 from the East-West Friendship Council received in 1944, must have been helpful – but only a very small proportion of the Mission's needs. The Mission's annual expenditure during these years is unknown, but it is bound to have increased because of the war-time demands and the children in the Mission's care. The subscription and donation list for 1943-1946 amounts to £1,519, which is about £30,000 at today's prices. Almost one-third of this, £477 had come from Learie Constantine, the world-famous West Indian cricketer settled in Lancashire. A total of £82 had come from African sources or donors with recognisably African names. Mr Keith had given £25 (apart from the £75 attributed to the Colonial Office on the list), the Methodist Missionary Society £24 and the Jewish League Refugee Committee £34. Even Liverpool worthies are on the list: the Bishop of Liverpool gave £1, the Lord Mayor two guineas (£2.10), and the Liverpool Council of Social Services £2/10/0 (£2.50).[18]

Self-help

Pastor Daniels did not only beg for assistance, he also helped himself: Mrs Roberts and her two daughters baked pies and apple tarts for the cafe and made toffee and toffee apples which were sold at the Mission. Stan Rogers, whose mother used to help in the Mission, remembers toffee being sold in the Mission's doorway. "There were large pans of toffee, cut with a knife. The Pastor sold pieces for a half-penny and did a roaring trade especially with the pupils from St. Patrick's close by." There was also a jumble sale once a month.

Mrs Roberts also cooked meals: these were free for those who could not afford to pay, while others paid a minimal charge.

Around 1940 or 1941, Pastor Daniels rented an old public house, the Conway Castle, on the corner of Park and Beaufort Streets, near the docks. Here he opened a cafe, the Cocoa Rooms. To cater to the dockers, the cafe was open from 5.30 am to 9 pm, and Saturday mornings. Mrs Roberts, her mother Mrs Blenkinsop, and one of Mrs Roberts's daughters worked there full time as well as keeping the Mission going and caring for the children. The other daughters still living at Hill Street had to help after work. Of the four daughters, Rita and Rose did the most work: "you either worked in Hill Street or the cafe... We used to do the baking at night, and early in the morning...the treacle tarts, and the cakes and pies. Even when we were still at school, we had jobs to do before we went to school. We were allowed a half hour play every day and one hour on Sundays... The dockers loved Pastor Daniels; he was well liked around here." The Pastor told

Ivor Cummings in October 1941 that "75% of the cafe's patrons are coloured people". Mr Cummings reported to the Colonial Office that the "dining room is run on hygienic and businesslike lines."[19]

Who were the patrons of the cafe? Mrs Charnod, who lived in the area at the time, remembers that it was used by the dockers as well as the locals. These 'locals did not include the Black families, though Black seamen just arrived at the docks did go there. "The cafe was very large. It had a big long table and benches, that way you could get more customers in. The people used to call the cafe the cloaker rooms. Mr Daniels sold simple food like chips, sausages and egg sandwiches. About three times a week he would put on potato meals and scouse –that was very special. (Scouse is a Liverpool regional dish.) There was also soup. The local people would go with a jug to get some, for sixpence. Everybody liked the chocolate cake. Mr Daniels was a gentleman in everybody's eyes, very polite and had a kind word for everybody."[20]

The cafe was closed in the early 1950s, possibly following Mrs Blenkinsop's death in 1953. Virtually the whole area was pulled down for redevelopment the following year.

In 1954, having lost the income from the cafe, Pastor Daniels applied to the City Council for planning permission "to use the Mission as a non-residential club with ancillary living accommodation". The Planning Officer recommended this change in use to the Committee of Highways and Planning. The Committee at first granted permission, but then for reasons not given, withdrew it. According to an officer in the Planning Department, this was very unusual.[21]

As if this setback were not enough, either in 1954 or in 1955 the Mission was vandalised and "thousands of pounds worth of damage was done to flooring, walls, stairs, windows and structural brickwork". All Pastor Daniels could salvage were two small rooms.

Despite these blows and the vast sums needed for repairs, Pastor Daniels persevered. He maintained his contacts with Africa: for example, in 1955 Mr J.O.C. Ojiako, Commissioner for Eastern Nigeria, visited the Mission. Pastor Daniels had appealed for funds and he had come in order to prepare a report for his government.[22]

Finally, as there had been, and still are, allegations that the Pastor used the Mission to enrich himself, the question has to be addressed: Did he? The answer is an unequivocal *NO*. The Pastor lived in semi-poverty all his years in Liverpool. He did not leave a will. No probate was ever granted. (When a person dies without leaving a will, the relatives have to request a probate for the distribution of the remaining possessions.) As no probate was ever granted, Pastor Daniels could not have left anything worth claiming. He died, as he had lived, a poor man.[23]

NOTES AND REFERENCES

1. Ethel Fegan, 'West African Girls in England', manuscript, n.d. (c.1937), p.11, Girton College: Ethel Fegan Papers. Daniels Ekarte to John Harris 21/4/1934, Rhodes House Library: Mss. Br. Emp. s.23, H1/21.
2. The postcards are in the possession of the Ankrah and Phillips families.
3. Daniels Ekarte to John Harris 21/4/1934 and Harris' reply 24/4/1934, Rhodes House Library: Mss. Br. Emp. s.23, H1/21.
4. On the relations between John Harris and Daniels Ekarte, see Carlton Wilson, 'Racism and Private Assistance', *African Studies Review*, 35/2, Sept. 1992. Also Wilson's A Hidden History: the Black Experience in Liverpool 1919–1945, PhD Dissertation, University of North Carolina, Chapel Hill, 1992, especially chapter 7. See also Paul B. Rich, 'Philanthropic Racism' (n.24, chapter 1).
5. Correspondence in Greenidge Papers, Rhodes House Library: Mss. Br. Emp. s. 19, E/8.
6. Wilson PhD (see n.4 above), p.408.
7. Lady Kathleen Simon had a long-standing interest in Black peoples. She was a member of the Anti-Slavery Society and the author of a book, *Slavery*, Hodder & Stoughton, 1929. Her husband Sir John, a Liberal, was Foreign Secretary and Chancellor of the Exchequer in the mid-1930s.
8. Letter from the Bishop of Liverpool, 19/11/1992. The Bishop did not reply to my request for the source of this suggestion.
9. Pastor G.D. Ekarte to the Under Secretary of State, Colonial Office 12/2/1937, enclosing a printed appeal for financial donations and 'Activities Report and Balance Sheet January – December 1936', PRO: C0847/8/11.
10. Minutes by Mr Sidebottom 26/8/1937 and O.G.R. Williams 26/8/1937, PRO: C0847/8/1.
11. John Harris to Colonial Office 22/10/1937, PRO: C0847/8/1.
12. Pastor Daniels Ekarte to the Under Secretary of State for the Colonies 25/1/1938, 30/6/1938 and 8/9/1938 and the replies, PRO: CO847/11/5.
13. Report by J.L. Keith on visit to the African Churches Mission 5/7/1941, PRO: C0859/76/9.

14. Report by Ivor Cummings on his and Paul's visit to the Mission 30/10/1941; R.B Paul to Keith 19/11/1941; J.L. Keith to Paul 10/12/1941; Keith to Daniels Ekarte 27/12/1941, PRO: C08591 76/10.
15. Correspondence Register PRO: C0977/1, file 11004/B4.
16. J.L. Keith to Mr Chance, Treasury 28/7/1943, PRO: C0876/38.
17. Correspondence Registers PRO: C0977/1-5, Files 11004/B4 for each year; Register CO977/10, file 11030/7; Register CO977/15, file 11076. The actual files have been destroyed and the Registers contain the briefest of entries, so it is impossible to be absolutely certain that the Mission's grants were stopped.
18. The African Churches Mission and Training Home, pamphlet, n.d. (c.1947/1948), PRO: H045/24265. The Treasurer was now Arthur Vanderpuje. (This name is sometimes spelled 'Vanderpuije'.) The donations of £50 for 1943-1944 and £75 for 1944-1945 from the East-West Friendship Council do not appear on the Pastor's list. They are noted in PRO: C0876/38.
19. Report by Ivor Cummings on his visit to Liverpool, 6/10/1941, PRO: C0859/76/10. I could find no trace of the cafe in Liverpool directories. Cafes did not have to register with any authorities in those days, so the Planning and other city departments have no information either.
20. Letter from Mrs V. Charnod to author, n.d. (c. October 1993.)
21. Correspondence 7/9/1992 and telephone conversation 11/12/1992 with the City Planning Officer's Department. The Committee on Highways and Planning accepted the Planning Officer's recommendation on 15/7/1954, but withdrew the permit "for further consideration" on 19/8/1954. No reasons are given in the City Council Minutes.
22. *Liverpool Daily Post*, 29/12/1955.
23. As Pastor Daniels died in a council flat, the city council would have had to ensure that proper procedures were followed.

CHAPTER NINE

The post-war years

After the loss of the children Pastor Daniels appeared to lose momentum. "Pastor Daniels and Mum were both devastated," Rose Phillips recalls. "We'd had them since they were babies. Rita and I were broken-hearted." Perhaps the anti-Black riots of 1948 added to his despondency.[1]

The character of the city's Black population changed again. Gone were the war-time 'Black Yanks' and many of the West Indian workers had returned home. But peace did not bring jobs to the colonies. Servicemen and workers who had returned to the Caribbean and Africa found the situation as hopeless as before the war. The resettlement programs were hopelessly inadequate. The most enterprising (and well off) bought tickets and set sail for Britain in search of jobs. Others arrived as stowaways.

In Liverpool, some of the welfare work had been taken out of the Pastor's hands. This had begun during the war with the appointments of Learie Constantine as Ministry of Labour Welfare Officer and of R.B. Paul as Port Welfare Officer. The League of Coloured People became active in the city especially on the Bishop's committee, which tried to raise funds for a new social centre.

The Colonial Office, undoubtedly pressed by these officials, as well as by the Bishop, Ian McLuckie at the University Settlement and the League of Coloured People, provided the funds to establish a community centre. Officially opened in 1946, the centre was named Stanley House, after the Secretary of State for Colonies. The Colonial Office also helped set up Colsea House, a segregated hostel for colonial seamen, which aimed to have the same standards as hostels for European seamen. With additional funding from the Save the Children Fund and the League, and with the secondment of a Leverhulme secretary to work full time for Stanley House, it was possible to start a nursery at 17 Falkner Square. In 1944 the nursery had 33 children, Black and White, in its care.[2]

It must have been a grave disappointment to Pastor Daniels that the Colonial Office had decided to bypass him when the decision was made regarding funding for Stanley House.[3] There is nothing in the remaining Colonial Office files to indicate why the Colonial Office decided not to build on the existing service being provided by the Mission. Was the Pastor seen to be 'too difficult?' After all, a man who demands equal wages for Africans, and who, for example, insisted that the Mission's Committee should be all Black, was clearly not a man who could be controlled easily. Could the Colonial Office not get involved in an organisation which was basically religious? Was there a fear that its religious nature would deter some people from using the centre? Did social class come into the government's calculations? Did the Colonial Office consider Pastor Daniels, whose formal education was limited, unsuitable for an enterprise as large as Stanley House? Or was the Pastor simply not able to work with committee structures?

However, despite the existence of Stanley House, in the late 1940s the Mission still functioned as both a religious and a social centre. Nigerian Philip Osisiogu, who arrived in Liverpool in 1948, remembers that "if you were Black and had problems, you went to Pastor Daniels and he took it up".

In 1953, free breakfasts were still served to the children. However, most of the work of the Mission had been suspended due to lack of funds, the Pastor explained to visiting Chief Kwabena Bonne III. In the same year the British sociologist Anthony Richmond, researching amongst Liverpool's Black population, wrote that "before the war there was a flourishing church... The church still exists but has not nearly the following it once had."[4]

In the mid-1950s, Jamaican Douglas Manley described the Pastor as "an aged man, a fundamentalist Christian." The building was in very poor condition. The Mission was still being used for meetings and services, but attendance was very small, sometimes a mere dozen. "The services were of a Protestant character with a strong racialist flavour but not very much emotionalism," Manley wrote. The Pastor was no longer involved in social, community or protest activities.[5]

In 1956 the Christian Missionary Society found the Mission's building derelict; once the children had been taken away, "work was virtually non-existent," the Society reported.[6]

But, despite his age and his inability to provide much, some people still valued Pastor Ekarte. When the Nigerian Union was started in 1957, Mr Ekarte was made the Union's patron. Some of the members would have liked to see him take a more active role, but he was prevented from doing so by a member who was involved in some illegal activities. "Pastor Daniels was against... He hated dishonesty... He did a lot for all the Africans. Until his death he fought for equality for Black people in Liverpool," Mr Osisiogu insists.[7]

Maybe there was just no place in this changing world for a man of Pastor Daniels's age, beliefs and style. The West Indians may have felt they were too 'sophisticated for the Mission and may have been attached to particular denominations. Many stopped going to church: Richmond found that though most West Indian immigrants had attended churches at home, in Liverpool "this habit of church attendance appears to have fallen off very rapidly."[8]

Africans were becoming involved in nationalism and the agitation for independence. Though Pastor Daniels retained a close and friendly relationship with the nationalists, at least one felt that "religion was not the right way to tackle the problem, because religion was used as a camouflage to bamboozle the black man." Occasionally the Mission still cropped up among the lists of those at political meetings. Thus in November 1949 the Pastor was among those demanding an independent commission of enquiry into the shooting of coal miners at Enugu, East Nigeria.[9]

In 1964 the Black-edited (and White-owned) *Flamingo* described the Mission building as "dilapidated, grim, tumble-down, its windows boarded up, its roof gaping with holes."[10] It could have held little attraction, and could provide few services to those seeking a better life in post-war Britain. The growing Black population was establishing its own diverse associations. In the post-war "Welfare State," some help was available from the local authority social services, housing and health departments.

By the order of the council, the building at 122-124 Hill Street was demolished in 1964. Pastor Daniels was moved to 27 Avison Terrace. Now a "white bearded, white-haired patriarchal" figure, he gave the impression of great age." He lived only a few weeks in his new home, until 12 July 1964.

Pastor Daniels was buried on July 20 in Allerton Cemetery. His unmarked grave has been identified as being Plot 115 in Church of England Section 8.[11] The *Liverpool Echo* published the tribute sent in by Matron Nella Armah of the Mother and Baby Home in Hoylake:

"I first went to his African Churches Mission the day it opened, when I was only a schoolgirl. Even then I realised here was a man prepared to devote his whole life to the welfare of others... He has been described as 'the African Saint and I can truly say that to a great many coloured people in Liverpool he was just that. Words can never describe the loss the coloured people have suffered by his death. He will never be forgotten among us."[12]

According to Mrs O'Brien, "Reverend Ekarte was such a kind man, my daughter used to say he might be God come to try and make the world a better place. We were Roman Catholic and we had every respect for this very kind gentleman."

The Mission did not die with the Pastor. After his death Mr Reginald Ankrah took it over and held services on the upper floor of the building at 64 Upper Parliament Street which housed the Nigerian Club. Mr Ankrah died in 1977 and another old parishioner, 'Chief' Osu took over.

In 1978 the Mission offered to sell the land at 122-124 Hill Street, but because of "legal difficulties... the purchase was never finalised." What these difficulties were, the Mission's solicitors could not determine as their office had burnt down in 1978 and all their records were destroyed.[13]

The land was finally developed by a local housing association into a block of flats in around 2005, without anything to indicate that it had once been a warm, caring and hospitable centre for the whole Hill Street community.

But the Black peoples of Liverpool, many no longer living in the South End, are continuing the fight for equality and against racism and discrimination. New organisations have sprung up, new – and old – battles are being fought. Some have made it through all the barriers and are administrators, teachers, lecturers, librarians, lawyers, social workers. Others are owners of art galleries, bookshops and small businesses. They have fulfilled the Pastor's dreams.

NOTES AND REFERENCES

1. On the 1948 riots see Michael Keith, The 1948 "Race Riots" in Liverpool, *Migration*, 13, 1992, pp.5-31.

2. Ian McLuckie had first got in touch with the Colonial Office when he was attempting to obtain a building for use as a centre for 'coloured seamen and Black US servicemen. Liverpool University Archives: Finance & General Purposes Committee of the Liverpool Settlement, Minutes 26/5/1943.
   Information on Stanley House nursery from: Lady Barton, 'A Group of Coloured Children,' *The World's Children*, September October 1944, p.97; Edward Fuller, 'Black and White,' *The World's Children*, July 1945, p.111; *Liverpool Daily Post*, 9/9/1946, 23/10/1943; *The Manchester Guardian*, 19/10/1943. See also PRO; C0876/43 (file 11004/42). The same file number exists for 1944.

3. The Stanley House building, in Upper Parliament Street, was bought by the Colonial Office, but had to meet its running costs from locally raised funds. In 1945 £2,500 was secured from the King's Fund for Sailors and The Merchant Navy Comforts Service. Liverpool University Archives: Settlement Minutes 20/6/1945. Stanley House was officially opened in September 1946. According to Jamaican researcher Douglas Manley, by the mid-1950s the warden "had little control...there was violence, drugs and prostitution.., Stanley House had little contact with other Black associations." (There were about ten at this time.) Manley also noted that the House's governing council was mainly White and that the first three wardens had been Whites. Douglas Manley, The Social Structure of the Liverpool Negro Community, PhD Dissertation, University of Liverpool, 1958.

4. *African Torchlight*, Winter 1953; *Liverpool Evening Express*, 1/7/1953. Anthony Richmond, *Colour Prejudice in Britain*, Routledge & Kegan Paul, 1954, p.96.
5. Douglas Manley (see note 3 above); Douglas Manley, 'The formal associations of the Negro community in Britain,' *Social & Economic Studies*, 4/3, 1955, p.241.
6. Church Missionary Society to the Anti-Slavery Society 7/12/1956, Rhodes House Library: Br. Emp. Mss. s.23, H3/3.
7. Interview and correspondence with Mr Philip Osisiogu, December 1992 and January-February 1993.
8. *Liverpool Echo* 23/7/1964; Anthony Richmond (see note 4), p.96.
9. Letter from Philip Osisiogu, 10/1/1993. CO: Register of Nigeria Correspondence 1949, file 30647/10/1.
10. *Flamingo,* August 1964, pp.11-12. The reporter was a local freelance journalist. I want to thank Marij van Helmond for this information.
11. Email from Allerton Cemetery to Terry Small, 21 March 2022. Thanks to Terry Small for obtaining this information and photographing the grave.
12. *Liverpool Echo*, 23/7/1964.
13. Letter from City Planning Officer 7/9/1992 and from Jackson & Canter, Solicitors, 8/10/1992.

Because so many records have been destroyed, the legal ownership of 122-124 Hill Street is a mystery. The application made in 1954 for permission to alter the use of the Mission to a "non-residential club with ancillary living premises" was submitted by Rollo & Mills Roberts (solicitors), on behalf of Mrs I.M. Xilaranious. I have been unsuccessful in my attempts to locate any information on this person.

APPENDICES

COLOURED AMERICANS' LEGACY TO BRITAIN
PROBLEM OF NEGRO G.I.'S CHILDREN

From George Padmore, London   **April 24th, 1947**

It is very encouraging to learn of the widespread sympathy among the American people for the unfortunate coloured children left behind in Britain by coloured G.I.s, not always through their own fault. It is a human tragedy that will always find a warm response from the generous American people; and it is all the more regrettable that an element of tendencious controversy threatens to becloud the problem.

A number of irresponsible statements have recently appeared in certain sections of the British Press from Correspondents in New York quoting interviews alleged to have been given to them by Mr. E.J. DuPlan, a native of the Gold Coast, West Africa, and a resident of Liverpool, England. Mr. DuPlan is the secretary of the Negro Welfare Centre which maintains a hostel for seamem in Liverpool and provides dances and other recreations for these seafarers while on shore.

However, I understand that Mr. DuPlan's mission in America is to raise funds on behalf of the African Churches Mission, a small religious community conducted in Liverpool by a very devout Christian gentleman, known as Pastor Ekarte, a native of Nigeria, West Africa. Mr. Ekarte maintains about ten to twelve coloured children in his Mission building which, unfortunately, has very limited facilities for the proper upbringing of his wards. Nevertheless, he is trying to do his best and enjoys the goodwill and support of a number of prominent British citizens interested in the wellbeing of the coloured children.

The reports which have appeared in the Press on both sides of the Atlantic are not only conflicting but, in the majority of cases, grossly untrue. It would appear that in order to dramatise the urgency of the problem, the total number of children has been multiplied at each interview. From my investigations, it would seem that the only authentic document on the problem of these illegitimate children born in Great Britain of English mothers and coloured American soldiers to have been issued is the survey made by a Jamaican social welfare worker, Miss Sylvia McNeill, under the auspices of the League of Coloured Peoples, 19, Old Queen Street, London, S.W.1. Until an official investigation has been instituted by the British Government, this document must remain the only authentic report extant on this problem.

Commenting upon this survey, Dr. M. Joseph Mitchell, General Secretary of the League of Coloured Peoples, estimated that the total number of such children does not exceed 1,700, and strongly condemns the alarmist reports which Mr. DuPlan is alleged to be making on the subject to the American public. For example, a report which appeared in the London Daily Mail of April 5, 1947, gives the utterly absurd figure of 10,000 as the number of coloured illegitimate children. Furthermore, this newspaper version quotes a statement made by one, Mr. E.A. Kendall, a British lawyer acting on behalf of Mr. DuPlan, to the effect that the United States Government has promised to send a liner to Britain in nine months' time to collect 5,000 of the children for transportation to the U.S.A., under the care of an expert staff of doctors and trained nurses. This report also goes on to allege that Mrs. Roosevelt is organising funds in America towards defraying the expenses involved.

From enquiries made in high official United States quarters in London, there is absolutely no confirmation of any such undertaking by the United States Government. When asked to comment upon the report issued by Mr. DuPlan's legal representative here, Dr. Joseph-Mitchell dismissed it as fantastic. "The Negro Welfare Centre and the African Churches Mission," explained Dr Joseph-Mitchell, "have only taken minor interest in this most important sociological work. What they seem to have done is to despatch Mr. DuPlan to the United States to appeal to the sympathies of the American people in an effort to extract money. It is a shame. It is a shame," emphasised Dr. Joseph-Mitchell, "that the work which is being done and which was originated by the League should be poached upon in this way just at a time when we have been able, through the American Embassy, to get the United States authorities to recognise their obligations to the children of G.I.s in this country.

"While Pastor Ekarte, an honest and sincere man, is struggling to do his best on behalf of the ten or twelve children for whom he has provided accommodation in his Mission hall, the League of Coloured Peoples, thanks to the generous support of British and American friends, has been able to establish a large and commodious institution known as the Rainbow Children's Home, where some 70 children are being cared for under the supervision of Mr. and Mrs. J.A.R. Russell and a band of volunteer English helpers. This is a mere fraction of the urgent and deserving cases of homeless children. Meanwhile, while contributing to the maintenance of the Home, the League of Coloured Peoples is endeavouring to raise additional funds to set up another home which can provide accommodation for at least a hundred children."

Turning to the question of adoption in the United States, where many people have expressed a desire to become foster parents to these unwanted children, and many of whom have written to Dr. Jospeh-Mitchell, he (himself a lawyer) explained to me the complicated international difficulties in the way of getting children transferred from Britain to America.

Expressing himself on this aspect, Dr. Joseph-Mitchell pointed out that while the British Government has not really interested themselves in the problem of these children, when the question of adoption by persons in America comes up, they insist upon investigating the circumstances of the intended foster-parents, their background, characters, financial position, and the rest. The children may be living in slums, totally wheared for and neglected, but the moment someone expresses a desire to adopt one or other of them, in steps the British Government. insisting that they shall not be handed over to foster-parents unless they can provide conditions to which they are not accustomed.

"The children," stated Dr. Joseph-Mitchell, "are subjects of King George, being born in the British Isles, and although it is possible for anyone in the United States to adopt a child, the requirements of English law are such that a number of formalities must be completed before the authorities in England will grant permission for the children to cross the Atlantic.

"In the first place, the consent of the Secretary of State for Home Affairs is necessary, and in the second place, the American Immigration Department will also have to grant its permission to each applicant. Moreover, a guardian must be obtained to accompany each child on its voyage from Britain to the United States." It will be seen from this that the question of adoption is by no means simple.

Checking up independently, I found from enquiries of a high authority at the Home Office, the equivalent of the American Department of the Interior, that the only organisations which the authorities in this country recognise and deal with on this problem of coloured illegitimate children are the British Family Welfare Association, headed by Mr. Asbury, O.B.E., who recently toured the United States lecturing on the problem of white women and coloured G.I.s in Britain, and the League of Coloured Peoples.

Through the activities of both these organisations, the United States Government have recently instructed Col. Alden E. Bailey, U.S. Army attache for Veteran Affairs, attached to the American Embassy in London. to co-operate with these organisations in giving assistance to the children of coloured veterans. I understand that under the provisions of the United States Veterans' Administration, wherever the League of Coloured Poeples can establish the paternity of young children, Col. Bailey's department in London will communicate with Washington advising the American authorities at home to allot "the appropriate share of any compensation, training or subsistence allowance, or any other type of benefit that the veteran may be receiving from the U.S. Veterans' Administration" for the maintenance of the child.

Now that this agreement has been established between Col. Bailey and the League of Coloured Peoples, Dr. Joseph-Mitchell is preparing a list of such claims from the well tabulated records which the League has been collecting over recent years. It is because of this careful study of the problem that the League of Coloured Peoples is the only organisation in this country with the facilities, as well as the staff, to undertake such work.

It is therefore most unfortunate if a false impression has been created in America because of Mr. DuPlan's statements, or those of any other person, regarding the true state of affairs in connection with coloured illegitimate children in Britain. The problem is urgent enough and requires the help, support and goodwill of all concerned about it.

But it is only fair to those who are interested that they should know that their contributions are not being misused by racketeers, but that they are going to the organisation which is honestly and sincerely endeavouring to cope with the problem and being used solely for the purpose for which they are given. In my view, on the basis of the investigation which I have made, the League of Coloured Peoples is the most reliable channel through which effective help can be rendered and contributions used for the welfare of these coloured illegitimate children until such time as the British and American Governments decide on a more official solution to a problem which is one of the sociological accompaniments of every war.

BASA NEWSLETTER #40
September 2004

A Reminiscence on Pastor Daniels Ekarte and the African Churches Mission

Thomas J. Jones

Something wonderful happened to me not long ago. A Mr Thomas Jones got in touch with me. Was I the author of the book on Pastor Daniels Ekarte? Yes. He had just read it, he told me. Had I known Pastor Daniels? No, I replied. His name was mentioned when I attended the planning meetings for the Transatlantic Slavery Gallery. As there were no books on him, I did a little research.... We talked and talked and I asked him to write down his memories of that remarkable Calabar man in Liverpool in the 1930s and '40s. 'I'm not a writer', Mr Jones reiterated again and again, but I think my arguing that he owed it to Pastor Daniels to write persuaded him... Here are excerpts, printed with Mr Jones' approval. This part of Mr Jones' memoir gives a wonderful (and so far unique) picture of services at the Mission. (The book is still available – from BASA at £6) The story will be continued in our next issue.

Recently on a trip to Liverpool I met an old friend, and during a discussion I mentioned I'd seen an article in a newspaper in London inviting people to vote for whom they thought should be honoured as the most outstanding British Black Man in Britain or British History.

How do voters measure being 'Most outstanding' or 'Great'? Is it by media publicity? Or is it just ignorance or lack of interest of Black history?

As we discussed the subject, I mentioned 'Daniels Mission' ; there was a big smile of approval and as far as we were concerned Pastor Daniels was a No1 candidate for any award, as he was not only outstanding, but a great man who not only helped people of his own race, but helped other ethnic races including white.

We were soon joined by another friend who happened to be the son of one of the organists that played at the 'Mission'. He asked us if we had read the book written about Pastor Daniels, and as we had not, he hurried away and returned with the book *Pastor Daniels Ekarte and the African Churches Mission Liverpool 1931-1964* by Marika Sherwood.

On returning to my hotel I began to read the book. It was a journey in time, and frequently I would wander off and the [?] would suddenly see the whole scene in my mind's eye like real.

I was taken by my father to the Sunday service at the African Churches Mission when I was about eight or nine years old, and after a while I joined the choir and Sunday became a really heavy day. There was Sunday morning service (compulsory for the choir), go home to dinner, return for the afternoon bible class or Sunday school; the choir stayed for tea as there wasn't time to go home because of the evening service. Mrs Morris used to make lots of cakes with jam on top and dipped in grated coconut.

(Even today, many, many years later when my wife buys similar but plain cakes, I jokingly ask, 'Where is the jam and coconut?)

A few of the congregation lived near by but most mainly lived some way away in the Upper Stanhope Street, Berkley street, and the top end of the Upper Hill Street area, nearer to the then tree lined Princes Avenue area which was some improvement, and a few families started to live beyond the Avenue. It must also be noted that most Black families moved to the area because there were more people like them and they would be a little safer from abuse by racist thugs.

Pastor Daniels had a natural feel for preaching and the congregation sang the hymns and Negro spirituals with great feeling, a feeling I've never heard or felt on the rare occasions of visiting other English churches. It was very similar in some ways to the Service in Black American Churches, very vibrant and Gospel style. Yes, Pastor Daniels was a natural and great preacher, who wasn't afraid of speaking out against the system. He was a man who only thought of helping people of all races, and that in itself was unique especially in that era of bigotry and racism in Liverpool.

Little did I realize that later in life I would be thankful for that short experience at the African Churches Mission, that spiritual feeling or 'Soul' that emanated though the congregation, would stay with you for a long time – it left a lasting memory in my life.

The choir was attired in black cassocks and white surplices and I'm sure, looked as smart as any other Church in the city. I remember there were two rows of choristers each side of the altar where Pastor Daniels preached, and a Mr. Ankrah was the organist and choirmaster. When Mr. Ankrah was absent his place at the organ was taken by a Mr. Bassey who was also one of the scoutmasters.

Even as I write these few words I can see the scene as we hurried to get our attire on. As we were the youngest, we had to take turns in carrying the cross at the head of the procession leading into the meeting room, singing songs of praise as we entered. The congregation would be in full singing voice, and those with deep voices loved to harmonize, making the place was very vibrant.

On most occasions it was a tight squeeze for the choir to get through between the people as there was usually a full house every Sunday.

There were serious moments and light hearted moments, Pa Daniels (as he was sometimes called by us,) had a subtle way of telling people they were doing wrong, or they should change their ways. He would stand up in the pulpit in true gospel style and denounce the sinners, but would never say their names.

We would be trying to contain ourselves from laughter because we all knew whom he was talking about. There was the time when he stood there arms bent on his chest grasping each side of his robes and referring to 'those who leave God's House and go to the house of Satan on the Sabbath day'. This resulted in us (the young lads) hiding our faces in the prayer book because we knew he was referring to Mr. Ankrah, the organist, who had a 'gig' (musicians term for an engagement) playing the violin at a dance that Sunday evening after church.

Sometimes the young lads would 'bend', the notes a little while singing; this would result in Mr. Ankrah, with head bent down raising his eyes towards us with a look of disapproval, but half smiling. We would ask him if we could jazz it up a little. This resulted in a group of about three or four of us attending his home for singing lessons. Unfortunately it only lasted a couple of lessons due to his wife being ill, and the group disbanded, and we still 'bent' the notes when the opportunity arose, and Mr Ankrah would raise his eyebrows once again.

Pastor Daniels had a hypnotic affect on his congregation at times, similar to the Black American Churches in the South, like people falling down and babbling strange words, or speaking in tongue. At first we (the boys in the choir) used to think one of the women who got affected a couple of times was trying to get noticed, but when other members in the congregation got affected we started to get a little concerned, especially if you were sitting at the end of the row near the people. Then a couple of the older members of the choir were overcome, one, a woman chorister on the opposite side, and the other, one of the men behind us.

Of course while this 'strange spirit' was circulating the room and the people were speaking in strange tongue, everything carried on as usual. Daniels preached and praised the Lord, the choir sang songs of praise, and the odd person said "halleluiah", with us young lads keeping a sharp eye on the congregation and nudging the next lad when someone collapsed to the floor.

Daniels preached about things which concerned the lives of the people, and many were having a tough time making ends meet, so it was easy for them to become emotional. Near the end of the service, Pastor Daniels would introduce the congregation to one or sometimes two seamen or stowaways who had been referred to him from different authorities who refused to help, and would ask if anyone in the congregation would help in providing accommodation until they could get some work. There were always volunteers who would take someone in.

There must be many grandchildren of these men around today; I wonder if they know about Pastor Daniels? I remember one of these men whom my family gave shelter to, eventually married a white woman with two children and went to live in Manchester where they lived very happily. You will also find other cases of White children brought up quite happily by Black fathers either by marriage or being abandoned by their parents, and these people must be grandparents today.

BASA NEWSLETTER #41
January 2005

A Reminiscence on Pastor Daniels Ekarte and the African Churches Mission

Thomas J. Jones

The beginning of this memoir of Liverpool in the 1930s was printed in our last issue. I have since learned that Mr Jones attended the London College of Music and became a drummer and band-leader. He played with many bands and eg at the Festival Hall, the Edinburgh Festival of Jazz and in many films. He was the producer of Cable Jazz on Cable London TV in the early 1990s.

The book (by Marika Sherwood on Pastor Ekarté) mentions activities in the Mission. There was the Boy Scouts, the Cubs, the Girl Guides, and the Brownies. There was also a 'Mothers Meeting', who went on trips to the seaside.

The Men, besides having a group singing spirituals, also had a cricket team which I remember were fitted out in all white cricket gear, this was besides the other activities mentioned in Marika Sherwood's book. It was the first time a black community ever had these activities organised for them in the whole of Great Britain never mind Liverpool.

I had never been to the mission in the afternoon during the weekday and I was soon to be initiated. It happened one day when I made the mistake of coming home from school for dinner and arriving dead on time, forgetting to allow the time it would take to walk home. My father looked at the time and commented "You're early, what happened"? He soon found out that I had played truant. For my punishment I had to accompany him to Pastor Daniels' Mission where I just sat down for a while in the recreation room watching the men playing billiards. We then went into Pastor Daniels' office and I had to sit and listen while they practised Spiritual songs like 'You got a shoe, I got a shoe, all God's children got a shoe', 'Some body's knocking at the door', 'Swing low sweet chariot', etc. They really sang with great feeling. Even at that young age I could sense a feeling of home sickness in these men when they sang an African song and Daniels would lead them in a little dance.

I made sure I didn't play truant from school again.

Pastor Daniels had a hypnotic affect on his congregation at times, similar to the Black American. Churches in the South, like people falling down and babbling strange words, or speaking in tongue. At first we choir the boys thought that the woman who got affected a couple of times was trying to get noticed, but when other members in the congregation got affected we started to get a little concerned - especially if you were sitting on the end of the row near the people. Then a couple of the older members of the choir were overcome: a woman chorister on the opposite side, and one of the men behind us.

Of course, while this 'strange spirit' was circulating the room and the people were speaking in a strange tongue, every thing carried on as usual. Daniels preached and praised the Lord, the choir sang songs of praise, and the odd person said "halleluiah", with us young lads keeping a sharp eye on the congregation and nudging the next lad when someone collapsed to the floor.

Daniels preached about things which concerned the lives of the people. Many were having a tough time making ends meet, so it was easy for them to become emotional.

The African Churches Mission was the centre of the black community in Liverpool. When people were desperate and had no one to turn to, or when destitute and hungry but refused help even by the African and West Indian Mission which was presided over by the Rev. Lawson but didn't help the needy, they would all end up at Daniels' Mission.

What made things more difficult was the extent of racism one would meet everywhere–period. In this era, racism existed wholesale and Pastor Daniels fought against it.

I remember a time when my mother gave me a shilling (5p) to buy a loaf of bread. I was about 9 years old.. Just ahead on the side of the road I noticed a group of older white boys. That was it, I knew trouble was coming. I immediately put the shilling piece

in my mouth and prepared for the worst. And it came. They crossed the road towards me. By this time was I outside the shop. One said "give us ye money" . Then the fireworks started, as they tried to grab me, I punched, slapped, and kicked one of them between the legs as there are no rules in the street. Then the old ladies started to shout "Leave him alone" and they ran off, and I carried on, bought my loaf of bread and went home. That episode was part of

The 348th Liverpool Scout Troop, the 'Liverpool Africans', 1935

every day life for a young Black kid growing up in Liverpool.

I knew then, that boys were brave in groups but cowards on their own. I also knew that these lads lived in the area and one day I would be walking with one of my friends and we would bump into one of them on his own and would proceed to teach him a lesson – a lesson which he never forgot. Now that sounds drastic to today's society but that's how life was lived in Liverpool at that time. Whenever you ventured out, you had to be ready to defend yourself. The worst thing you could do was to show cowardice or that you were afraid.

Another time, when coming home for dinner from the service in the Mission with my father, a group of older white boys gathered on the where we lived. I'd seen them from a distance and started to get a little apprehensive, because I'd seen them before knew they were going to make racial remarks, and my father like the rest of the community was not going to stand for any insults.

I now started to imagine this episode as a military offensive: my father was the 'Commanding Officer' , and I waited for the order to take up position. Then the offensive started, and I was ordered to change position from inside to the outside, which left the Commanding Officer between the enemy and me. As we advanced nearer to the position of engagement one of the enemy remarked "f-cking bl..". But he never got further than "bl.." when there was a 'whooshing' sound as the Commanding Officer's Walking stick travelled through the air in their direction, and returned to inflict further 'whooshes' through the air as they scattered.

Suddenly the area of engagement was clear, everything was serene and back to normal, and we continued on our way home with the troops (me) resuming position to the inside.

The result of this attitude eventually paid off and they began to pay us more respect. When both sides met on foreign soil, for example in the Merchant Navy, in which many men of both sides served, when they realised they were from the same city, they would come to each other's aid when in trouble. Gradually both sides grew up together as you will find in Toxteth today.

In my time in Liverpool, Black kids grew up with rules like:

The Cubs, uniforms not yet supplied

1. If you want a job, you have to be better than your white counterpart, not the same, but better. That was your only chance of getting the job..

2. If you were a boxer, then don't bother about winning on points, knock him out or forget it.

These rules applied to everything you did, may it be sports or the arts, you had to work that little bit harder. There are a lot of businesses which will give you work if they know they are getting better quality for the same price.

Apart from these hazards there are a lot of wonderful people in Liverpool who will treat you with respect, and I'm sure others like me have met and worked with many, but the fight for equality still goes on. In my recent visit to the city, the majority of the present generation seemed to have changed for the better, except for the newspaper reports of hooligans at some football matches.

To be continued.

BASA NEWSLETTER #42
April 2005

A Reminiscence on Pastor Daniels Ekarte and the African Churches Mission

Thomas J. Jones

The first two sections of this memoir of Liverpool in the 1930s were printed in the previous two issues.our last issue. If you want to know more about the author's subsequent life, look him up in the *International Who's Who in Music*. Mr Jones asked that we add a footnote to the last episode, to point out that 'All disputes, fights and bullying were settled with fisticuffs. The use of knives was very rare, and nobody possessed guns.' We pick up Tom Jones' life in 1936, when he was ten years old. (This memoir was written in response to Marika Sherwood's book on Daniels Ekarte, which is available from BASA for £6)

The Mission's Choir

There would be times when one of Pastor Daniels' choir would oversleep or was missing for some reason. Then Daniels would take the choir round to their place of abode and pray and sing a hymn for their recovery.

What a wonderful thing is the power of prayer, as they would emerge from their homes looking the worst for no sleep and apologizing for being late. We young lads found it hard to stop ourselves from laughing at the situation when they emerged, because Daniels wouldn't give up and they had to come out.

There were times when some unsuspecting soul would emerge from their home, still half asleep on their way to work, and would think they were watching a 'holy apparition', and stood transfixed. One man said 'of my god, ghosts', and rushed back in.

This escapade was more than hymn-singing around the local streets, we would venture into the city. Oh yes, Daniels was a cute man, he knew what he was doing! He was demonstrating, was trying to bring to the attention of the public the plight of the Black community, the same people who fought in wars and gave their lives for them, only to be cast aside when they had served their purpose. We ended up outside St.George's Hall in Lime Street between the two stone lions in front of the building. Besides demonstrating our existence to 'Joe Public', he was giving us a history lesson by telling us how the city had made its money in the past: that all within this precinct including the statutes of the slave traders, was built out of the riches made in the Great Liverpool Slave Trade.

Suddenly the newspaper boy started to shout 'Paper', 'King George V dies'. Upon hearing this, Pastor Daniels said a prayer, asking the Lord to accept him into heaven. As it was early in the morning and all the preachers, clergymen, etc were all in their beds asleep, it was the one and only Pastor Daniels Ekarte who was the first to pay homage to the old King. We then returned to the mission singing songs of praise on the way.

That was one of the most memorable occasions of my being in the choir.

Of the Imitation of Christ

Pastor Ekarte was one of the three transcribers of the First Book *Of the Imitation of Christ* by Thomas à Kempis into the Calabar language, which was printed by the Mission in 1934. Not only is this book probably one of the first books translated into an African language in Eastern Nigeria, but it gives and insight into the advanced thinking of Pastor Daniels at that time.

Of the Imitation *of Christ* is a collection of four books, said to have been written in the 14th century by two or three members of 'The Brethren of the Common Life', a Dutch brotherhood. It was transcribed into Latin by Thomas à Kempis (1380-1471), who was educated by the Brethren and joined their community. The books are filled with instruction and inspiration for the student of mystical philosophy. Essentially a spiritual diary, the book has remained, after the Bible, the most widely read book in the world.[1]

Maybe early subconscious training at Daniels' Mission is the reason why I have found it easier to read and interpret that type of subject, which is now more common in the western world since George Harrison of The Beatles introduced many people to eastern philosophy and meditation.

I gradually stopped going to the Mission as we moved further away and I got older. But the experience stays with you.

Pastor Daniels' other work

I remember Pastor Daniels taking in the children born to Black American Servicemen because nobody would help with the 'problem'. These children would now be in their sixties and are most probably grandparents. Are they keeping their life story a secret from the children? Most of all, do they spare a thought or even remember Pastor Daniels Ekarte and his African Churches Mission, the 'Angel of Toxteth', who came to their rescue and fought for their survival?

Special mention must be given to Mrs Roberts (Mrs Morris) and her daughters, who must be highly commended for the work they did in the Mission. Looking after the children must have been a nightmare as I don't remember anyone in the community offering to help, and it seemed to be people form outside that helped. There has to be some soul searching here.

Liverpool and the police

The mention of 'disreputable clubs' is ridiculous. The community had no entertainment of their own, and it was appreciated and necessary for someone to open a place of some kind of entertainment, rather like the working men's clubs. Today this type of accusation would be frowned upon.

It seems the authorities didn't like the community enjoying itself. I remember a musician organising a Saturday dance only to be raided by the police and sentenced to 18 moths imprisonment for holding an indecent dance. This 'indecent dance' was later described as the 'jitterbug' or 'jiving', a dance still performed today, and awarded prized in the BBC series 'Come Dancing'.

After WWII

After being discharged from the Merchant Navy I moved to London and started to make a living as a musician. Whenever it was possible, or when working with a bank, I would take a trip to Liverpool. On occasion I would bump into my old choirmaster, Mr Ankara from Pastor Daniels' Mission, who was always interested in my progress.

It was a sad day then I heard that the authorities had taken the Mission from Pastor Daniels and ordered it to be demolished and moved him to a terrace flat, where he died after a few weeks.

In the history of Liverpool I have never heard of any one person who has helped his fellow man like Pastor Daniels Ekarte. He has earned the privilege of some kind of plaque erected in his memory. Surely, Liverpool, the 'European Capital of Culture' can afford it!

[1] Thomas à Kempis *Of the Imitation of Christ*, International School of Theology, www.leaderu.com/cyber/auther.html

Outings with the
Mothers' Union

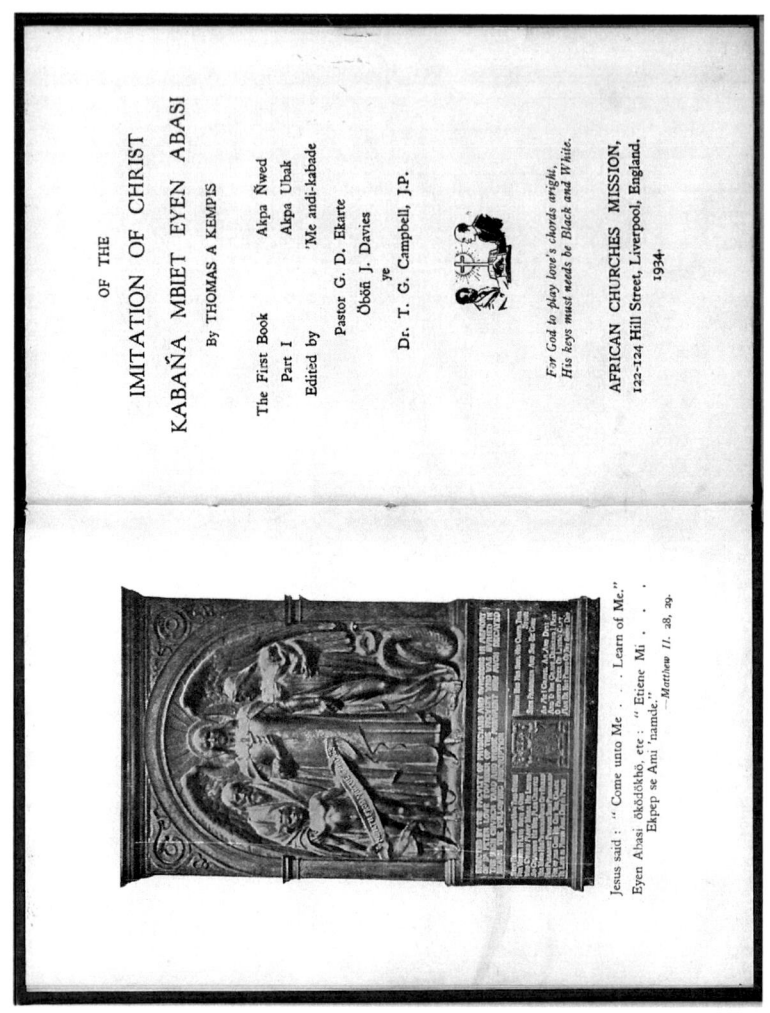

The frontispiece and title page of a book co-translated into Ibibio by Pastor Daniels and Mr. J Davies. From the collection of Ms. Bernadette Akpan.

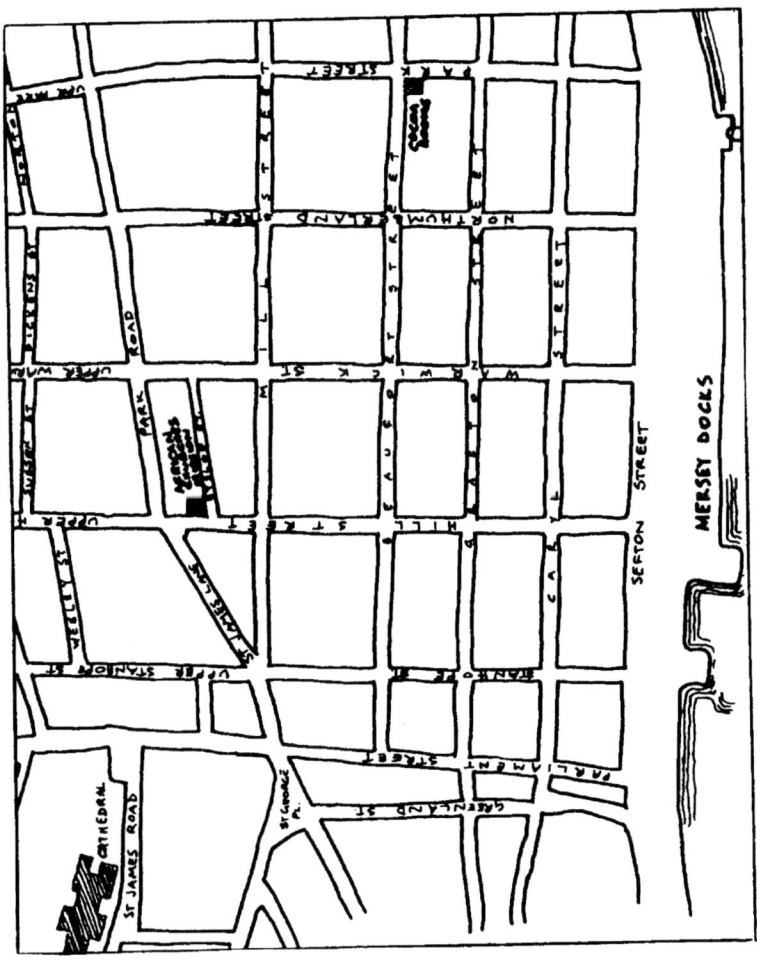

Hill Street area, 1934 (main roads only)

THE AFRICAN CHURCHES MISSION.

TELEPHONE:	MISSIONER:	122/4 HILL STREET,
ROYAL 5210	G. DANIELS EKARTE.	**LIVERPOOL,**

21st, April 1934

W O R K I N G   C O M M I T T E E.

G. B.	Thomas,	Esq;	(Chairman)	E. Daikens,	Esq;
A.	Wenton,	,,		J. Tennyson	,,
B.	Williams	,,		T. Bassey	,,
V.	James	,,		J. Dixon	,,
Geo,	Okon	,,		J. Lewis	,,
J. A.	Olawumi	,,		J. Davies	(Hon,Sec,)

Pastor G.D.Ekarte, Missioner.

The
African Churches Mission
& Training Home.

Rev. G. DANIELS EKARTE, Founder and Pastor-in-charge.

E.A. MENSAH, Eqs., General Secretary

Dr. STUART McAUSLAND, M.D., M.R.C.S., Hon. Physician.

136

The
African Churches Mission
& Training Home.

The Aim or Object.

———

1 To promote and extend the adoption of the Mission principles among the Negroes and their children in the City, and its environs.

2 To improve the general condition and protection in the interest of all members.

3 To provide Funds for the relief of members when in distress.

4 To provide a special heartiest voluntary work among the children and the interest in self-respect among the struggling, oppressed, scattered and dispersed negroes in the world.

5 To provide funds for the training of the children in the highest education which is the medium by which people are prepared for the creation of their own particular civilisation and the advancement and glory of their own race.

6 To provide Funds for the Training of the children in Commercial, Agricultural, and other Industries. (Please see page 7).

7 To maintain a placement bureau through which qualified members in any particular industry can obtain a post to Africa, their Fatherland.

8 To endeavour to obtain reasonable hours of duty and fair wages for the seafaring workers, and to use every legitimate effort to provide for their safety.

9 To abide in the determination to propagate the doctrine of Jesus Christ, which is based on the principles of Peace, the Brotherhood of man and the Fatherhood of God, and to prove abundantly the blessing which will result from its practical observance.
"Go ye therefore ....!"
— *St. Matt. XXVIII. 19-20. St. Mark XVI. 15-20.*

✝

The
African Churches Mission
and Training Home.

122/4 HILL STREET, LIVERPOOL 8.

"Friends of All—Enemies of None."

●

President—
REV. E. A. EJESA-OSORA. M.A.

Vice President—
BISHOP A. B. AKINYELE, D.D.

Chairman—
VICTOR JAMES, Esq.

Pastor and Superintendent—
G. DANIELS EKARTE.

Hon. Treasurer—
ARTHUR VANDERPUIJE, Esq.

Hon. Secretary—
ADSETE SOWA, Esq.

Representatives in Africa.
AMATE SOWA, Esq.
Teshi, Gold Coast

DR. THOMAS ABELS,
Sapele, Nigeria

138

The African Churches Mission,
122-24, HILL STREET,
LIVERPOOL, 8.

Members of the Black Race, Friends and Sympathisers of other Races:

You are cordially invited to attend the SPECIAL

REMEMBRANCE - DAY
SERVICES,

on behalf of the Aborigines' Rights Protection Society of West Africa, on

Sunday, 11TH October

1936, at 11 a.m., 3 p.m. & 7 p.m., when Prayers will be offered for the Progress of the Society both at home and abroad.

PRINCIPAL SPEAKER :

GEORGE PADMORE, Esq., of London.

CHAIRMAN :

Pres. GEORGE SMITH, Esq.,
of the Gold Coast Aborigines' Society, Liverpool.

The body of the Liverpool Branch of the Society will be present in full force.

Rev. G. D. EKARTE will conduct the Meetings.

COME ONE, COME ALL ! A GREAT DAY AWAITS YOU.

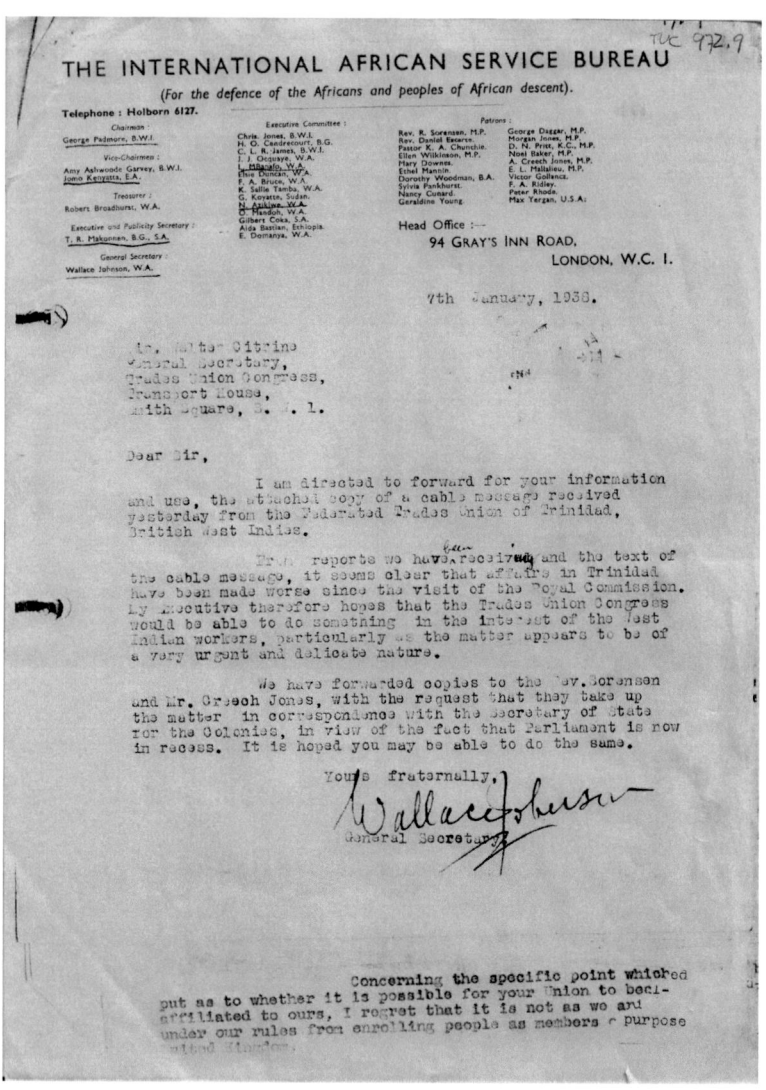

TUC 972.9

THE INTERNATIONAL AFRICAN SERVICE BUREAU

(For the defence of the Africans and peoples of African descent).

Telephone : Holborn 6127.

Chairman :
George Padmore, B.W.I.

Vice-Chairmen :
Amy Ashwoode Garvey, B.W.I.
Jomo Kenyatta, E.A.

Treasurer :
Robert Broadhurst, W.A.

Executive and Publicity Secretary :
T. R. Makonnen, B.G., S.A.

General Secretary :
Wallace Johnson, W.A.

Executive Committee :
Chris. Jones, B.W.I.
H. O. Ceandrecourt, B.G.
C. L. R. James, B.W.I.
J. J. Ocquaye, W.A.
L. Mbanefo, W.A.
Theo Duncan, W.A.
F. A. Bruce, W.A.
K. Sallie Tamba, W.A.
G. Kovatts, Sudan.
N. Azikiwe, W.A.
O. Mendoh, W.A.
Gilbert Coka, S.A.
Alda Bastian, Ethiopia.
E. Domanya, W.A.

Patrons :
Rev. R. Sorenson, M.P.
Rev. Daniel Escarto.
Pastor K. A. Chunshie.
Ellen Wilkinson, M.P.
Mary Downes.
Ethel Mannin.
Dorothy Woodman, B.A.
Sylvia Pankhurst.
Nancy Cunard.
Geraldine Young.

George Dagger, M.P.
Morgan Jones, M.P.
D. N. Pritt, K.C., M.P.
Noel Baker, M.P.
A. Creech Jones, M.P.
E. L. Mallalieu, M.P.
Victor Gollancz.
F. A. Ridley.
Peter Rhode.
Max Yergan, U.S.A.

Head Office :—
94 GRAY'S INN ROAD,
LONDON, W.C. 1.

7th January, 1938.

Mr. Walter Citrine
General Secretary,
Trades Union Congress,
Transport House,
Smith Square, S. W. 1.

Dear Sir,

I am directed to forward for your information
and use, the attached copy of a cable message received
yesterday from the Federated Trades Union of Trinidad,
British West Indies.

From reports we have received and the text of
the cable message, it seems clear that affairs in Trinidad
have been made worse since the visit of the Royal Commission.
My Executive therefore hopes that the Trades Union Congress
would be able to do something in the interest of the West
Indian workers, particularly as the matter appears to be of
a very urgent and delicate nature.

We have forwarded copies to the Rev. Sorenson
and Mr. Creech Jones, with the request that they take up
the matter in correspondence with the Secretary of State
for the Colonies, in view of the fact that Parliament is now
in recess. It is hoped you may be able to do the same.

Yours fraternally,

Wallace Johnson
General Secretary.

Concerning the specific point which ed
put as to whether it is possible for your Union to beci-
affiliated to ours, I regret that it is not as we and
under our rules from enrolling people as members r purpose
ited Kingdom.

The Pastor is listed among the Patrons, but his name is mis-spelled

1972   calendar   1972
AFRICAN CHURCHES MISSION
LIVERPOOL

Motto : FRIENDS FOR ALL, ENEMIES FOR NONE

Sunday Meetings
Morning Service 11am
Evening Service 6 pm
Sunday School 2.30 pm

Weekly Meetings
Tuesday: Choir Practice
Thursday : Prayer and
Choir Practice

Rev. Daniel Ekate
FOUNDER

Chapel: **64 UPPER PARLIAMENT STREET, LIVERPOOL L8 7LF**

All correspondence to: Rev. Reginald Ankrah, 39 Upper Parliament Street, Liverpool L8 7LA

JANUARY 1972

Sun	Mon	Tue	Wed	Thu	Fri	Sat
						1
2	3	4	5	6	7	8
9	10	11	12	13	14	15
16	17	18	19	20	21	22
23	24	25	26	27	28	29
30	31					

FEBRUARY 1972

Sun	Mon	Tue	Wed	Thu	Fri	Sat
		1	2	3	4	5
6	7	8	9	10	11	12
13	14	15	16	17	18	19
20	21	22	23	24	25	26
27	28	29				

MARCH 1972

Sun	Mon	Tue	Wed	Thu	Fri	Sat
			1	2	3	4
5	6	7	8	9	10	11
12	13	14	15	16	17	18
19	20	21	22	23	24	25
26	27	28	29	30	31	

APRIL 1972

Sun	Mon	Tue	Wed	Thu	Fri	Sat
						1
2	3	4	5	6	7	8
9	10	11	12	13	14	15
16	17	18	19	20	21	22
23	24	25	26	27	28	29
30						

MAY 1972

Sun	Mon	Tue	Wed	Thu	Fri	Sat
	1	2	3	4	5	6
7	8	9	10	11	12	13
14	15	16	17	18	19	20
21	22	23	24	25	26	27
28	29	30	31			

JUNE 1972

Sun	Mon	Tue	Wed	Thu	Fri	Sat
				1	2	3
4	5	6	7	8	9	10
11	12	13	14	15	16	17
18	19	20	21	22	23	24
25	26	27	28	29	30	

JULY 1972

Sun	Mon	Tue	Wed	Thu	Fri	Sat
						1
2	3	4	5	6	7	8
9	10	11	12	13	14	15
16	17	18	19	20	21	22
23	24	25	26	27	28	29
30	31					

AUGUST 1972

Sun	Mon	Tue	Wed	Thu	Fri	Sat
		1	2	3	4	5
6	7	8	9	10	11	12
13	14	15	16	17	18	19
20	21	22	23	24	25	26
27	28	29	30	31		

SEPTEMBER 1972

Sun	Mon	Tue	Wed	Thu	Fri	Sat
					1	2
3	4	5	6	7	8	9
10	11	12	13	14	15	16
17	18	19	20	21	22	23
24	25	26	27	28	29	30

OCTOBER 1972

Sun	Mon	Tue	Wed	Thu	Fri	Sat
1	2	3	4	5	6	7
8	9	10	11	12	13	14
15	16	17	18	19	20	21
22	23	24	25	26	27	28
29	30	31				

NOVEMBER 1972

Sun	Mon	Tue	Wed	Thu	Fri	Sat
			1	2	3	4
5	6	7	8	9	10	11
12	13	14	15	16	17	18
19	20	21	22	23	24	25
26	27	28	29	30		

DECEMBER 1972

Sun	Mon	Tue	Wed	Thu	Fri	Sat
31					1	2
3	4	5	6	7	8	9
10	11	12	13	14	15	16
17	18	19	20	21	22	23
24	25	26	27	28	29	30

Posthumous calendar from the collection of Ms. Bernadette Akpan, daughter of Mr. William Akpan, former seaman, and friend and "countryman" of Pastor Daniels, from Calabar.

CHURCH OF
ENGLAND SECTIONS
7, 8, 11 & 12
SECTION 11.
SECTION 12.
SECTION 7.
SECTION 8.

Garden of Remembrance
Springwood Crematorium
JEWISH SPRINGWOOD
Mortuary Chapel
Springwood Avenue
Woolton Road
Hillfoot Road
Brunt Lane
Chapel
YARD

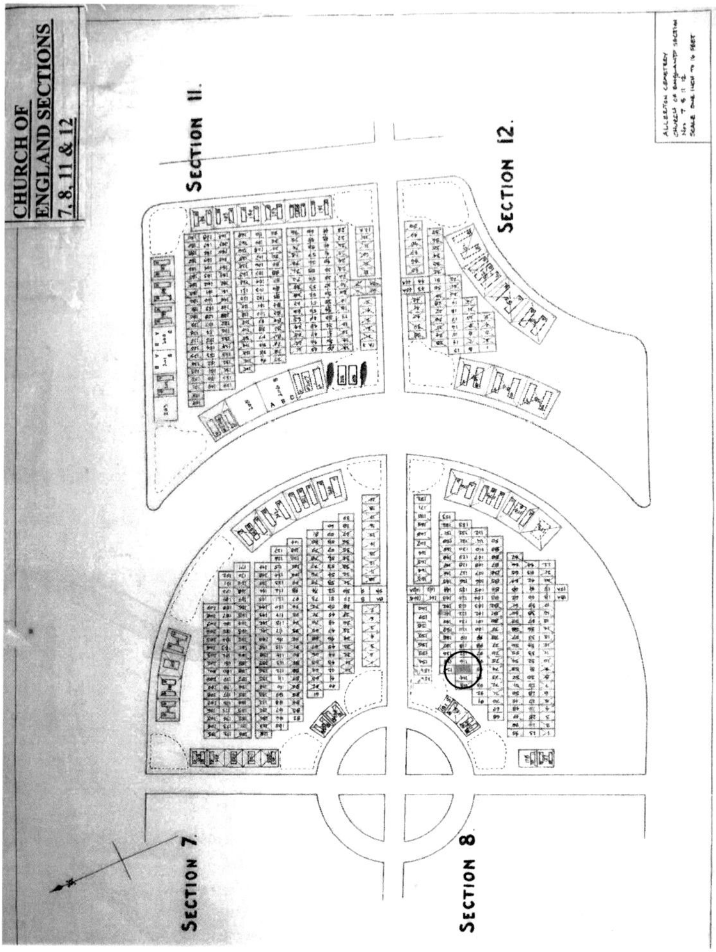

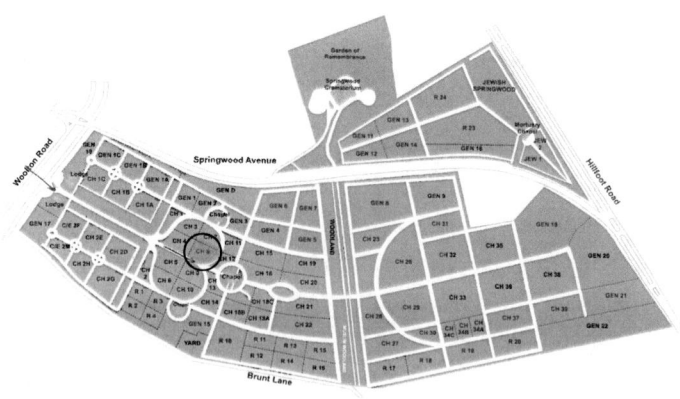

Stephen Small's brother, Terry Small, contacted the Allerton Cemetery and paid the required fee for them to locate Pastor Daniels Ekarte's unmarked grave. In April 2022, he visited the cemetery and took the above photographs of the grave site. *(Photos courtesy of Terry Small)*

Facing page, top: Aerial view of Allerton Cemetery indicating the location (circled) of Pastor Daniels Ekarte's unmarked grave.

Facing page, bottom: The unmarked grave (circled) is located in Section CH 8, grave number 115.

INDEX